The Power and Weakness of God:
Impassibility and Orthodoxy

Papers presented at the Third Edinburgh Conference in
Christian Dogmatics, 1989

edited by
Nigel M. de S. Cameron

With best wishes,
Paul Wells

RUTHERFORD HOUSE BOOKS
Edinburgh

Published by Rutherford House, 17 Claremont Park,
Edinburgh EH6 7PJ, Scotland

SCOTTISH BULLETIN OF EVANGELICAL THEOLOGY
SPECIAL STUDY 4

ISBN 0 946068 43 7

Computer typeset at Rutherford House on Apple Macintosh™

Printed in Great Britain by
Billing & Sons Ltd, Worcester

Dr Nigel M. de S. Cameron is the Warden of Rutherford House, Edinburgh.

Henri Blocher is Dean and Professor of Systematic Theology in the Faculté de Théologie Évangelique, Vaux-sur-Seine, Paris, France.

Dr Peter R. Forster is the Senior Tutor at St John's College, Durham.

Paul Wells is the Professor of Systematic Theology in the Faculté de Théologie Réformée, Aix-en-Provence, France.

Dr E. David Cook is the Director of the Whitefield Institute and a Fellow of Green College, Oxford.

Richard Bauckham is the Reader in the History of Christian Thought, at the University of Manchester.

Paul Helm is the Reader in Philosophy, at the University of Liverpool.

The cover illustration depicts the crucifixion from J. Fleetwood's *Life of our Blessed Lord and Saviour Jesus Christ*, 1857.

Contents

Preface

The papers which follow were read at the third in the series of two-yearly, international theological conferences to be convened at Rutherford House. Earlier conferences (with papers also published in this series) addressed theological method (published in 1987 as *The Challenge of Evangelical Theology*) and the problem of faith and history (*Issues in Faith and History*, 1989). As we go to press, the fourth conference is in preparation for 1991, with as its twin *foci* universalism and the doctrine of hell.

The aim of the conference is to bring together the best in evangelical theology – theological thinking which is both orthodox (faithful to Scripture) and fresh (faithful to the Holy Spirit and the questing theological task of the church). These two qualities are not always found together; indeed, their divorce is perhaps the commonest feature of contemporary theology, whether 'liberal' or 'conservative'. It is our prayer that these papers, like the two volumes which have preceded them, may in some measure move us forward in our search for the truth on such fundamental questions.

The Edinburgh Conference in Christian Dogmatics is one among a number of theological projects through which Rutherford House has sought to catalyse theological activity. Another is the related Rutherford House Fellowship, which brings together some one hundred scholars engaged in evangelical theological research. Another is the Rutherford Studies series, which publishes serious monographs in contemporary and historical theology. Another is the *Scottish Bulletin of Evangelical Theology*, which plays host to this supplement series. Another – the most recent – is the *European Journal of Theology*, edited across many countries, which we hope will be brought to the birth in 1991. The House's work centres on a residential library, and encompasses other journals (in theology and also in bioethics) and long-term research projects (a new edition of Calvin's Old Testament commentaries and the *Dictionary of Scottish Church History and Theology*). Yet the central concern for fresh, orthodox evangelical theology – and for its publication – is nowhere better evidenced than here.

We commend these papers, both to scholars and to pastors, for they seek to address one of the central mysteries of our faith in a manner which is responsible to the 'given' of our theology in Christ and in Scripture, and also to the anguished reflection to which doing justice to what is given inevitably leads. There are no short-cuts to the truth, however firmly we may believe we know where it lies. And that is true nowhere more than here, where we tread on such very holy ground.

Nigel M. de S. Cameron
Rutherford House, Edinburgh
April 1990

DIVINE IMMUTABILITY

HENRI BLOCHER

Deuteronomy 29:29

Is Heracleitus, at last, getting his revenge over his old rival Parmenides? During 2,000 years, Being, immutable Being, successfully claimed the Lion's share; it was enthroned on high. Becoming had to be content with the lower end of the scale, inferior earthly reality. Becoming was reckoned as degraded Being. But a complete reversal has taken place. Now, the *Umwertung*! The epithet 'static', which suits Being, has become distinctly pejorative. Dynamically to be on the move now holds supreme value.

Many factors have come into play in modern history to bring about this reversal. The new power of man over his environment, with its enormous effects on the way, and means, of life, has changed the perception of time: no longer primarily the agent of decay, but the bearer of *progress*. One consequence of a raised standard of living has been equalization and democracy, with a political mood hostile to the *status quo* understood as old inequality defended by the privileged few: *revolution*, which is superlative change, has appealed to many indeed, including theologians. At a deeper level, the preference for Becoming may stem from the *promotion of the human subject*: when creative man, endowed with chameleon-like freedom (Pico della Mirandola), stands at the centre, or, rather, moves at the head of the world, change is more esteemed than fixity.

Theology mirrors the change about change. Classical Christian theology had followed in the footsteps of Philo, the father of technical theology, whose treatise on Genesis 6 bears the eloquent title: *Quod Deus immutabilis sit.*

1

After Nicaea, which threw an anathema at those who say that the Son is *treptos* or *alloiôtos*, Augustine most forcefully celebrated God as unchanging and unchangeable. Later orthodoxy followed in his train, on the Protestant as well as on the Catholic side. The French Reformed Confession of faith (de la Rochelle), in which Calvin himself had a share, explicitly mentions in its first article the attribute of immutability. In the mid-nineteenth century, however, the climate was no longer the same; in the introduction to the long study he devoted to the theme, originally published as articles in the *Jahrbuch für deutsche Theologie* (1856–58), Isaac Dorner spoke of a wave of dissatisfaction with the traditional views.[1] Many, since, have denounced, or even derided, them as pieces of Greek philosophising, alien to the true biblical religion.[2]

It appears that theological debates today concentrate less directly on immutability than they did in Dorner's time, and more on impassibility and omnipotence. Will not the issue of God and change divert us from the main agenda: reflecting on the power and weakness of God, examining the thought of the suffering God? Actually, these questions are interlaced, and the common objection to divine *passions* is that passions would involve *changes* in the Godhead. To both mutability and passibility, dogmatic tradition opposes that God's absolute *power* excludes any dependence of God on anything or anyone beyond himself: hence, that he cannot be *affected*. Thomas

---

[1] I.A. Dorner, 'Ueber die richtige Fassung des dogmatischen Begriff der Unveraenderlichkeit Gottes, mit besonderer Beziehung auf das gegenseitige Verhaeltniss zwischen Gottes uebergeschichtlichem und geschichtlichem Leben', in *Gesammelte Schriften aus dem Gebiet der systematischen Theologie, Exegese und Geschichte* (Berlin: Wilhelm Herz, 1883) pp. 199ff.

[2] Emil Brunner, in his *Dogmatics I*, xx, par. 1 & 2, comes very close to such a charge, but wishes to maintain that God is unchanging from another point of view: see *Dogmatique I*, tr. into French by Frédéric Jaccard (Geneva: Labor & Fides, 1964) pp. 293f, 297.

Aquinas stresses that there is no *potentia* in him, since he is *actus purus*:[3] François Turretin, that there is no *potentia passiva*.[4] And if the topic of immutability, in spite of all these connections, is found to be slightly off the centre, it may helpfully vary our perspective. The problem of time and eternity is also very close at hand, as already set forth in Philo's work,[5] and most insistently by Augustine.

We would distinguish three levels into which we must inquire. First, we should try to ascertain whether God changes or not, or, if he does, how and in what measure. Second, we should dig a little deeper and consider the underlying issue of God's relationship to his creatures, as to dependence. And then, the more speculative question of the import of the incarnation for God's being, God's *trinitarian* being, cannot be avoided in the present theological context. Inevitably Moltmann!

Even before that, it will be wise for us to clarify the proper means of our endeavour: a first, preliminary, section will lift corners of the veil from our methodological options.

Sign-posts of Method
The first recommendation is this: we should refrain from the abuse of *symmetry*, especially in facile *antitheses*. James Barr has freed us from common stereotypes of the Greek and Hebrew minds – but they are still a temptation, and we should beware of backsliding! More generally, binary thinking, such as deals only with two alternatives,

---

[3] *Summa theologiae*, Ia Qu. 9, art. 1, 2.

[4] *Institutio theologiae elencticae* I (New York: Robert Carter, 1847) p. 185 (Quest. xi).

[5] *Quod Deus sit immutabilis*, par. 32, Greek text and French tr. with notes by A. Mosès, *les Oeuvres de Philon d'Alexandrie*, ed. by Roger Arnaldez, Jean Pouilloux & Claude Mondésert, vol. 7–8 (Paris: Cerf, 1963) pp. 78ff; in par. 31, Philo calls God the grand-father of time, since he is the father of the universe, which is the father of time (pp. 76f).

3

mutable/immutable, may be too simple. Logically, *tertium non datur*, but are we sure that, under each of the terms, *several* possibilities are not to be discerned? In some cases, courage requires that we cut through a crude either-or; but in others, wisdom is on the side of caution and flexibility.

Our *principium cognoscendi externum* is Scripture, the Word of God. As we rest on this secure ground, we deplore any bondage of theology under the dictates of human philosophy. Indeed, we become easily critical of past generations: we are amazed that they could imbibe so naïvely Platonic prejudices – obvious axioms to them. Let the one who stands .... Too zealous an attempt to remove the ontological speck from our fathers' eyes should make us suspicious of ourselves! We are in danger of falling into the *same* trap – on the other side. Philosophical certainties are rare commodities, and we should remember their frailty. In an aging culture, with a rich memory of countless superior minds refuted by other superior minds come after them, an ounce of Pascalian scepticism does seem a lesson taught by historical experience.

In all vigilance, therefore, let Scripture be our teacher, the totally trustworthy teacher. *Both individual statements and the trends* which reflect biblical sensitivities should guide us, symphonically: no part despised, however small, and unity believed.

Classical theology has interpreted many of the relevant statements of Scripture as figurative language. Scripture speaks pedagogical, or even *medical*, untruth in Philo's explanation;[6] at least *metaphorice* for Thomas Aquinas;[7] *anthrôpathôs* for Turretin.[8] The danger is here acute that

---

[6] *Ibid.*, par. 63ff, pp. 94ff.
[7] *Summa theol.*, Ia Qu. 9, art. I, ad 3m.
[8] *Institutio I*, p. 186.

4

the authority of biblical pronouncement be neutralized in the interests of alien presuppositions. Reacting against Augustine and Quenstedt, Emil Brunner exclaims: 'Have not the prophets and the apostles spoken of God *digne* or *proprie*?'[9] This gives food for thought – but it may also border on cheap rhetoric! For we cannot deny that Scripture, at least on occasion, does use anthropomorphisms!

How can we detect the presence of such? Contradiction with other statements, if taken literally, is evidence which corresponds to the standard method with metaphors. Any hint of a metalinguistic kind, in the text, may also help. The tone and style of the context will increase or lessen probabilities, especially if we can ascertain the writer's intent or *scopus*. We shall do well, however, to leave a wide margin for doubt.

While listening to Scripture, we shall pay attention to the great events it witnesses to. But woe unto us if we dare substitute for the divinely-inspired teaching of God a direct use (that is our own thinking) of the events – whether we call it 'hermeneutics' or not! A theology of the genitive, choosing this or that event as *the* key of theologising, not only runs the risk of distorting the shape and meaning of the events, but it transmutes their concrete singularity into *abstraction*. There is something sorely disturbing in the 'freedom' in which some have been indulging of late. Creation, Incarnation, the Cross, the *eschaton*, are not ideas for us to play games ... We are but disciples at the feet of the Master.

A humble posture will also imply the right attitude towards *tradition*. In order to allow the authority of Scripture its free course, no tradition should play a magisterial role; but a *ministerial* role, yes, indeed.

---

[9] *Dogmatique I*, p. 261 (introduction to chapter 17).

Basically, tradition is a blessing. Reverence is fitting on our side. Only afterwards shall we be so bold as to criticize and to correct.

Concretely, tradition means traditions. We shall be consistent with our commitment of faith if we privilege the tradition of the Reformers, as embodied in the continuous line of evangelical dogmatics.

Scripture on Balance
When one has just read Philo or Thomas Aquinas on divine eternity and immutability, the first shock in Scripture is the liveliness of the biblical God. He is the mobile God who acts and reacts, the God who utters threats and withdraws them, the God who turns from wrath to grace, and also chastises with frightening blaze those who betray him among his chosen people.

The second shock, however, comes, in contrast with much modern writing, when we realize that the affirmation of God's unchangeableness spreads its roots far and wide in all Scripture. *It is a biblical theme*, and not a minor one at that! Thomas Aquinas is content to quote one proof-text, Malachi 3:6 (not the strongest one, maybe, although not without force); theological forefathers nearer to us, Turretin and Charles Hodge, set forth remarkable biblical summaries; they really sound as if the fruit of their tactful and erudite exegesis were the ground of their conviction, rather than philosophical or speculative considerations.

Most definite statements are found in Numbers 23:29, 1 Samuel 15:29 (is *nétsah* a title for God in his perpetuity?), and James 1:16f. All three involve a contrast with creaturely mutability; James richly elaborates this thought, implying a 'critique' of the variations of luminaries (more or less divinised in paganism). How could one dream of a better *sedes doctrinae*? 2 Timothy 2:13 also evidences special cogitation of the same sort.

6

Throughout Scripture, as Raphael Schulte indicates, the first orientation of our theme is ethical; yet, 'the deeper reflection on God's being is not lacking; rather, it is acknowledged as the foundation of the unchangeableness of God, *i.e.* of his unshakable faithfulness to himself, and, then, of his dealings with men'.[10] Psalm 102:24ff is the other development which stems from a deep meditation, unmistakably metaphysical, with eternity and immutability interlocked.

The grand *'attâ-hû'* in the Psalm finds its counterpart in the triumphant *'anî-hû'* of Moses' song (Deut. 32:39) and of the proclamations in Isaiah (41:4; 43:10,13; 46:4; 48:12). A possible paraphrase of YHWH, the LXX generally renders it I AM. The comment of Brown, Driver and Briggs is worth-quoting: *'i.e.* He Who *Is* (as opposed to unreal gods named in context, or to the transitory world), the Unseen, yet Omni-present, and Self-Consistent Ruler of the world'.[11]

Other pointers abound. The beloved metaphor of the 'Rock' also tells of immutability. The Lord is praised for the unchanging firmness of his designs and promises (Ps. 33:11; Prov. 19:21; Is. 46:10; especially Heb. 6:16ff); he differs from the fickle deities of the heathen, and equally fickle humankind. In the New Testament, 'incorruptibility' and 'immortality' are ascribed to God (1 Tim. 6:16), and they are very close to immutability in their Greek comprehension (Rom. 1:23; 1 Tim. 1:17). Even more broadly, the biblical mind values permanence, stability, that which cannot be moved — whereas the godless are like a changing sea (Israelites were not fond of ventures at

---

10 'Unveraenderlichkeit Gottes', in Josef Hoefer & Karl Rahner, ed., *Lexikon fuer Theologie und Kirche*, (Friburg: Herder, 1965) X: 536.
11 Francis Brown, S.R. Driver & Charles A. Briggs, *A Hebrew and English Lexicon of the Old Testament* (Oxford: Clarendon, 1906) p. 216b.

sea!) and like chaff in the wind. Truth, *'èmèth*, means solidity forever (Ps. 119:160).

Such a harvest of data seems to rule out any flat denial of divine immutability. Only a low estimate of Scriptural authority can accommodate the views expressed under the flag of Process Theology and Philosophy: especially when it appears, as Colin Gunton shows in Hartshorne's case, that the 'changeless' aspect of deity is but its complete openness to change.[12]

Are we, then, to go back simply to the older position? The explanation of 'God repented' as figurative speech may well claim support from the character of the diction, and from the warning of Numbers 23:19 that we should not understand the phrase literally. But is the same true when the language of varied activity, of transition from enmity to peace, is used, even in didactic material? Dorner is not satisfied when 'it is said with illustrious teachers from Augustine to Schleiermacher, [that] it is only the receptivity of the world which varies, [that] that receptivity is the cause of the seeming variety in the divine presence, [that] it receives the various impressions from the God who is equally presented to everything...'.[13] Charles Hodge himself, with edifying frankness, considers Quenstedt's words as greatly 'open to objection' when the great Lutheran scholastic states that divine immutability 'negates absolutely any movement whatsoever, whether physical or ethical'; Hodge complains that theologians have been 'apt to confound immutability and immobility. In denying that God can change, they seem to deny that God can act'; although Turretin was more cautious than Quenstedt, Hodge is not

---

[12] Colin E. Gunton, *Becoming and Being. The Doctrine of God in Charles Hartshorne and Karl Barth* (Oxford: O.U.P., 1978, rep. 1980) p. 34; on p. 33: God is eternal *as* all-temporal.

[13] J. [*sic*] A. Dorner, *A System of Christian Doctrine I,* tr. into English by Alfred Cave (Edinburgh: T. &T. Clark, 1880) p. 245.

convinced by Turretin's exclusion of any 'variation of God's internal acts'; he comments on this clause that it 'assumes a knowledge of the nature of God to which man has no legitimate claim'.[14] One fears that the augustinian argument based on divine perfection – any change would make it imperfect – suffers from an analogous presumption: from too hasty an application of our logic to the mystery of *God's* perfection.[15]

On the 'twin' topic of God's *eternity*, classical theology is found in a position even weaker: biblical support is hard to find for the axiom of the pure timeless present, the *nunc aeternum*. Dorner makes a strong point when he claims: if that axiom be valid, 'then history is mere appearance, and devoid of valuable result';[16] the Atonement is robbed of its effect on divine displeasure, the heart of the Gospel is at stake.[17] The contemporary logician Peter Geach concurs, and goes even as far as saying: 'If time and change are only apparent, not real, features of the world, Christian (or Jewish or Muslim) theism is altogether destroyed';[18] he rightly sees that time is not real if it is not real *for God*, although Geach wishes to retain Boethius' definition of eternity.[19]

Sic et Non? Is it possible to hold together both the 'liveliness' and the immutability of God, as many dream they could? We may not 'water down' divine unchangeableness and reduce its difference with creaturely variation to a mere matter of degree. Moltmann, once,

---

14 Charles Hodge, *Systematic Theology* (New York: Scribner's, 1870) I: 391.
15 Repeated by Turretin, *Institutio I*, p. 185.
16 *System I*, p. 246.
17 Dorner, *System of Christian Doctrine IV*, tr. into English by J.S. Banks (Edinburgh: T. & T. Clark, 1882) p. 33.
18 Peter T. Geach, *Providence and Evil* (Cambridge: Cambridge U.P., 1977) p. 42; *cf.* p. 57.
19 *Ibid.*, pp. 43 and 130.

seems to play with this feeble solution; he declares his agreement with Nicaea that God does not change, and he comments: 'But that statement is not absolute; it is only a simile. God is not changeable as creatures are changeable'.[20] Moltmann adds, however, the idea that God is free to change himself and to let himself be changed by the other person;[21] the whole problem is 'how?'. Dorner admirably sets the theologian's goal: 'The satisfactory dogmatic formula will only be found in that which permits both, the divine Immutability and Vitality, to be so regarded as one, that God may be living just by virtue of the fact which gives him His inviolable Immutability, and conversely'.[22] He triumphantly goes on: 'And this fact is given in the ethical idea of God peculiar to Christianity, in the correct idea of love' – God's 'ethical essence'.[23] But if one avoids, as Dorner is careful to avoid, a disastrous sundering of the ethical from the metaphysical in God, have we gained more than another way of stating the same problem?

Many would join Dorner as he makes one further step and admits 'historically regarded, a changing action and relation of God to the changing world', while God remains *'internally* self-identical'.[24] *God-for-us* changing and changeable; *God-in-himself* immutable. Luther, already, in a *scholium* on Romans 3:5, exclaimed: 'God is changing to the highest degree ... See Psalm 18 (v. 27): "With the man of election, Thou art a God of election; with the man of diversion, Thou usest diversion". As a man – any man – is in himself, so is God for him as he confronts him .... To be

---

[20] Juergen Moltmann, *The Crucified God*, tr. into English by John Bowden and R.A. Wilson (London: S.C.M., 1974) p. 229; 'a simile' seems to mean that it is a matter of comparison only (p. 216 in the original).
[21] *Ibid.*, pp. 229f.
[22] *System I*, par. 32, p. 460.
[23] *Ibid.*
[24] *Ibid.*, p. 461.

true, this change is external to God (*haec mutatio extrinseca est*)'.[25]

This construction may well be the best model on the table, the one which best fits the biblical complexity – although the emphasis in Scripture falls on God's unchangeableness *in his relations with us*. Yet, for theological intelligence, it goes little beyond Hodge's frank avowal of mystery! For *who* is the God-in-relation if not the God-himself? If *he* does not change, the relationship which varies reduces to a *semblance* of involvement for *him*. And if he does, how can his *'anî-hû'* and James 1:17 still hold?

The Creator and his Creatures
What emerges as the cardinal issue is the character of God's relationship with other agents. If we affirm the Absolute, the Self-Sufficient, Independent, Lord, it is fairly easy to attribute unchangeableness to his nature; but we find it difficult to involve him truly in a relationship, and even to make room for the *reality* of other beings – we sail into the Charybdis of a mere semblance of a world, of such an emptying of the substance of creaturehood that there can be no partners to God, but only vanishing shadows on the brink of nothingness. If we reverse our choice, and imagine a dependent God, who has to reckon with causes that function autonomously, not entirely subject to divine decision, mutability clearly proceeds: such a God had better change to adapt himself to the moves of his partners! But does he still deserve to be called God? We make shipwreck on the Scylla of deity reduced to humanity writ large. God stands as one among many agents (and patients), though he may be the first; he strives to do his best, and he often fails; he attracts our sympathy, maybe

25 From the French tr. by R.H. Esnault, in *Oeuvres de Luther*, vol. XI (Geneva: Labor & Fides, 1983) p. 311, corresponding to the Weimar Ausgabe, 56, 234.

even our commiseration. There is no fear of God in that land...!

However praiseworthy the wish to steer a middle course between appalling excesses, half-measures provide no adequate solution. Many fall a prey to the fallacy of myopic cosmomorphism. Within the universe, within the solidarity of created being, dependence and independence are always a matter of *degree*, and there can be a mixture of both. But there cannot be a *measure* of independence from God. If something or someone is independent from God, there is no reference for measurement, no principle over-arching, no category, no space, in which the two can be *together*: unless there be a God beyond God, a higher and truly all-embracing God! Actually, no confrontation is even thinkable!

Some writers, even apart from Process theologians and from extreme liberals, have come to deny God's foresight of the future, in spite of the massive evidence of Scripture to the contrary.[26] Peter Geach is too wise for such a drastic departure from biblical doctrine; he correctly says: 'I am not denying that God is omniscient about the future; I think God knows the future by controlling it'.[27] Yet, because of an emotional reaction against Jonathan Edwards' statements, he would not allow God to determine in any way the decisions of men: 'God cannot be surprised or thwarted or cheated or disappointed' only because he plays chess so much better than the other players.[28] But a move independent of God is not found on the same chess-board with God's! It has *nothing in common* with God. It is absolutely wild, indomitable.

---

[26] *E.g.*, the 'Evangelical' historian Pierre Chaunu, *Ce que je crois* (Paris: Bernard Grasset, 1983) p. 192 (pp. 173f, 182f).
[27] *Op. cit.*, p. 57.
[28] *Ibid.*, p. 58; cf. pp. 61, 137 (against Hobbes who had refuted an Arminian).

To avoid polytheistic chaos, the temptation is then to make the independent finite (?) cause *a part of God*. It remains independent in the sense of absolute self-determination, but it is a moment, or an aspect, of the divine life. Since Krause, who coined the word, such a scheme goes by the name of *panentheism*. But it is hard to see how it really differs from a timid version of pantheism. An internal distinction in 'God' is woefully inadequate against the pantheistic threat. Spinoza's pantheism *also* differentiated between *Natura naturata* and *Natura naturans*. Hartshorne's dipolar deity, whose concrete pole is the world, for whom (for which) he revives the Stoic theme of the world-soul, is no freer from cosmic entanglement.[29] In Paul Tillich's brand of panentheism, as it is well-known, Being-itself, the depth and power of being *in* all beings, has no real distinction from the world. In all pantheistic directions, lies the insuperable difficulty of accounting for the difference that remains: how can the One be dipolar?

Nicolas Berdiaeff, with Moltmann's apparent approval, discerns that monism and dualism cannot escape each other, and he concludes that we should combine them dialectically.[30] But are not, then, dialectics a way to cover up failure, and a double distortion, from both sides? The Dooyeweerdian diagnosis of such dialectics as the symptom of the heart's bondage to an idolatrous antinomy should protect us from the charm of dialectical magic. Moving endlessly to and fro between Charybdis and Scylla does not bring one much nearer to Paradise.

---

[29] *Op. cit.*, especially pp. 42, 70; also 21, 29, 34, 37, 57, 70f, 81.
[30] Juergen Moltmann, *Trinité et Royaume de Dieu. Contributions au traité de Dieu*, tr. into French by Morand Kleiber (Paris: Cerf, 1984) p. 65; we did not have access to the English translation, *The Trinity and the Kingdom: The Doctrine of God*, tr. by Margaret Kohl (San Francisco: Harper & Row, 1981).

The revelation of our God throughout Scripture explodes any possible doubt. The Lord's independence is proclaimed. Not only does Paul definitely state that God has no need of anything (Acts 17:25), as Psalm 50 already implied, but the majesty of his lordship, the related titles and *theologoumena* produce an overwhelming impression. The *Pantokratôr* of John the Seer is the Pauline blessed and only Ruler, the King of those who reign, the Lord of those who govern, who alone has immortality (1 Tim. 6:17f), of whom, through whom and for whom are all things, who is the *'anî-hû'* of Isaiah, who is the God of the whirlwind in the theophany granted to Job, who is the LORD. He does not depend on his creatures. His creatures depend on him, even in their response to him: he works in the faithful, according to his good pleasure, that they will and that they do (Phil. 2:13). In the case of the creatures' *evil* response itself – which introduces the *other*, opaque, mystery – Scripture on several occasions declares that God in some way *determined* beforehand that they would thus turn against him (Acts 4:27f; Ezek. 14:9, *etc.*). The biblical Lord so dominates his relationship to his creatures that 'it does not depend on the man who wills or on the man who runs, but on God who has mercy': for 'Who resists his will?' (Rom. 9:16,19).

When God, in Scripture, is calling men to decision, and taking with utter seriousness their choices and moves, we read nowhere that men, then, decide independently of him. The praise of God's patience, as he holds back his righteous anger (as he delays his judgement), never suggests a self-limitation or contraction of God, *zimzum*, in order that creatures may *be*, and may be *free*. This old cabbalistic doctrine, of which Moltmann has grown so fond,[31] seems entirely foreign to the revelation of him 'in

---

[31] Ibid., pp. 141ff; also Juergen Moltmann, *Dieu dans la création. Traité écologique de la création,* tr. into French by Morand Kleiber (Paris: Cerf, 1988) pp. 120ff; English translation, *God in Creation:*

whom we live, we move and have our being'. Even Zeus –
for whose sake these words were first composed – did not
enjoy the biblical Lord's supremacy. Abraham Heschel,
the very thinker who has been so influential by exalting
the divine *pathos*, witnesses to the unparalleled force of
the divine lordship in Scripture:

> To the Biblical man, God is the supreme Lord who
> alone rules over all things. This association of the
> concept of God with the idea of absolute sovereignty
> and supreme power may be contrasted with other ways
> of religious thinking. Zeus, for example....[32]

At the same time, beyond all question, God does take with
utter seriousness the choices and moves of men. Precisely
as he rules over the world and *judges* it, the difference
between God and the world shines out and dispels all
ambiguity. A foundational duality comes to fulfilment in the
duality of Covenant (and its 'dipleuric' aspect). Against all
pantheistic understanding of creaturely dependence,
Heschel relevantly notes that 'divinisation' is foreign to
biblical religion.[33] Man has reality for God, and yet, 'the
relationship between God and man is not dialectic'.[34]

The original Jewish thinker gives us a clue which may
help us find a better way. Heschel uncovers the root of the
Greek philosophers' predicament, which he labels 'the
ontocentric predicament'. For them, being is first and last:

> The acceptance of the ultimacy of being is a *petitio
> principii*; it mistakes a problem for a solution. The
> supreme and ultimate issue is not *being* but the
> *mystery* of being.[35]

An Ecological Doctrine of Creation, tr. by Margaret Kohl (London:
S.C.M., 1985).

[32] Abraham J. Heschel, *The Prophets II* (Harper Torchbooks; New
York, *etc.*: Harper & Row, 1962, 1975 paperback) p. 18.

[33] *Ibid.*, p. 49.

[34] *Ibid.*, p. 9. Heschel's concern is to avoid a strict antithesis, and he
uses 'dialectic' in that sense, which is not entirely the same as ours.

[35] *Ibid.*, p. 43.

The mystery of being is that of its source and origin, he explains: *creation*. Instead of the natural world, theology finds its starting-point in God, the *semper agens*; it tells of his acts, before asking about being.[36] This insight may free us from the dilemma of monism and dualism dialectically opposed or related. *The starting-point, taught by Scripture, is the Creator-creature pattern.* We cannot raise ourselves higher and dominate the constitutive structure, we cannot subsume it under an all-embracing notion of being. It involves a real duality, non-symmetrical: absolute independence on one side, total dependence on the other. The obedience of faith, in receiving this orientation as the principle of sound thinking, does not boast that it has solved the monistic-dualistic antinomy, but humbly *refuses* it. For the antinomy is worldly: its reference is the world of the autonomous self; we should probably discern that it stems from the prior refusal of the divinely revealed pattern.

With this pattern, however, in-forming, refashioning from within our vision, it may be easier for us to accept that God in himself changes not, and, yet, can put real interest in his Covenant-partners, and share in the movement of their history.

We cannot rise above the Creator-creature relationship, but God has told us of his own life, and of the revelatory function of his creation. We are not exalting ourselves beyond measure if we inquire about the ground or foundation in God himself of his creative work. Several among the masters have seen in the *trinitarian* differentiation of the Godhead the archetypal ground for the differentiation between God and the world. Karl Rahner thus formulates this suggestion:

The ontological possibility of creation can derive from and be based on the fact that God, the unoriginated,

---

[36] *Ibid.*, p. 44.

expresses himself in himself and for himself and so constitutes the original, divine, distinction in God himself.[37]
Karl Barth has pointed to the same derivation.[38] It is by no means a twentieth century novelty. Even Heschel, with a degree of embarrassment, comes not very far from the Kingdom of the Trinity when he writes: *'God*'s being One means more than just being one'![39]

Scripture appears to lend support to the thesis, mainly in the passages which are indebted to Proverbs 8 and Wisdom christology. In turn, the proposition brings to bear on the mystery of immutable life the light of a linkage with the *other* mystery of God, the mystery of the Three-in-One.

Incarnation and the Trinity

If we try to associate the question of divine immutability to the Trinity, a more obvious connection arrests us. At the centre of the economic Trinity, the incarnation: God (the Son) *became* man! If ever there was an event which implied *change* for God, it must have been the incarnation.

Two of the most inventive among the theologians of our time have scrutinized the issue. Karl Rahner has propounded provocative suggestions in his typical manner, both respectful of tradition and daringly modern.[40] Jürgen Moltmann, who wages war against 'monotheism' (correlated with political despotism and patriarchal

---

[37] Karl Rahner, 'On the Theology of the Incarnation', in *Theological Investigations IV*, tr. by Kevin Smyth (Baltimore: Helicon, and London: Darton, Longman & Todd, 1966) p. 115.

[38] See Eberhard Juengel's emphasis and interpretation in *The Doctrine of the Trinity. God's Being Is in Becoming*, tr. cop. Scottish Academic Press Ltd (Grand Rapids: Wm B. Eerdmans, 1976) p. 99.

[39] *Op. cit.*, p. 47.

[40] In the essay quoted above, note 37: (first published in *Catholica*, 1958).

sexism), has attempted to draw a doctrine of the Trinity from the Cross of the Son.

Moltmann's *Crucified God* puts forward the boldest statements. 'Anyone who really talks of the Trinity really talks of the cross of Jesus, and does not speculate in heavenly riddles'.[41] 'The Trinity is no self-contained group in heaven, but an eschatological process open for men on earth, which stems from the cross of Christ'.[42] 'We have not just seen one person of the Trinity suffer in the event of the cross, as though the Trinity were already present in itself, in the divine nature'; in the event, the 'persons constitute themselves in their relationship with each other'.[43] Moltmann calls for a 'complete reshaping' of trinitarian theology in which 'the nature of God would have to be the human history of Christ and not a divine "nature" separate from man'.[44] He faces the consequences:

> the unity of the dialectical history of Father and Son and Spirit in the cross of Golgotha, full of tension as it is, can be described, so to speak retrospectively, as 'God'. ... In that case, 'God' is not another nature or a heavenly person or a moral authority, but in fact an 'event'. ... In that case, is there no 'personal God'? If 'God' is an event, can one pray to him? One cannot pray to an 'event'. In that case there is in fact no 'personal God' as a person projected in heaven. But there are persons in God: the Son, the Father and the Spirit. In that case one does not simply pray to God as a heavenly Thou, but prays *in* God.[45]

'In that case' refers plainly to the actual state of affairs in Moltmann's view.

---

[41] *The Crucified God*, p. 207.

[42] *Ibid.*, p. 249 (*cf.* p. 255: 'not a closed circle of perfect being in heaven', but a 'dialectical event').

[43] *Ibid.*, p. 245.

[44] *Ibid.*, p. 239.

[45] *Ibid.*, p. 247.

Such powerful language would seem to leave no possibility of misinterpretation, nor of any affirmation of the eternal immanent Trinity, as distinguished from the economic Trinity. However, Moltmann presents his readers with little surprises. Although, to our knowledge, Moltmann never retracted his previous utterances, in more recent writings he does go back to the immanent Trinity *ab origine*. He seems to agree that the original order is the *foundation* in God for the missions *ad extra*, of Son and Spirit.[46] Can he be credited with perfect consistency? He still prefers to speak of a 'trinitarian history of God', he still tries to balance a constitution 'from the end' with the constitution from the origin,[47] and he still keeps the cross at the centre of the Trinity – with an appeal to the common misreading of Revelation 13:8.[48] He now favours a reciprocal determination of essence and revelation (or economy), allowing for a priority of influence of God's relationship to himself over his relationship to the world.[49]

Whether in harder or softer forms, Moltmann's view of the cross-event as a constitution or, at least, an essential reshaping of the divine Trinity, creates severe problems for the evangelical student of theology. Apart from the highly disputable use of a few passages, it cannot lay claim to any biblical support. As a matter of fact, the later *Shekinah* speculations of some traditions within Judaism seem to have played a more decisive part than Scriptural discipline in Moltmann's inspiration here. Dependence on Hegel is no secret, with the same tendency to transmute into *concepts*, with which dialectical reversals and abstract

---

46 Juergen Moltmann, 'L'Absolu et l'historique dans la théologie de la Trinité', in *Hegel et la théologie contemporaine*, ed. J.-L. Leuba & C.-J. Pinto de Oliveira (Neuchâtel and Paris: Delachaux & Niestlé, 1977) pp. 193f.

47 *Ibid.*, pp. 196ff.

48 *Trinité et Royaume de Dieu*, p. 202.

49 *Ibid.*, pp. 203f.

generalisations follow, the concrete events of the Gospel: in spite of high-flown 'concreteness' rhetoric! Rahner has detected in it an 'essential gnostic tendency', and we should hear this judgment as a solemn warning.[50]

The force of Moltmann's argument really hinges on his rejection of the Chalcedonian two natures. He obviously distastes the distinction in the Symbol: unconfusedly, unchangeably.[51] For him, the *human* history of Jesus enters God's being and thus determines Trinity. *We* would maintain the Chalcedonian scheme as not only indispensable if deity and humanity are to be confessed with their Scriptural value, but, as such, already discernable in the New Testament. The logic of Hebrews 1 and 2, and of Paul in Romans 9:1–5, so implies; less distinctly, but still truly, do the developments in Philippians 2, Colossians 1:15ff, even Romans 1:3f. The structure of John's prologue reflects careful reflection on the precise point. Turretin's reply to those who argued for divine mutability on the basis of the incarnation, that the *Person* of the Son, the *Logos*, became flesh, took on human nature, and not *deity* as such, has solid biblical foundations.[52]

Et tamen... Rahner's comment that, while this *is* valid, we are still left with the fact that the *Logos* became flesh, that he was God and *became* something different, hits the nail also.[53] The suggestion he, then, draws, may improve upon the one we tended, provisionally, to receive: 'If we face squarely the fact of the incarnation..., we must simply say: God can become something, he who is unchangeable

[50] Karl Rahner, *Le Courage du théologien. Dialogues publiés par Paul Imhof et Hubert Biallowons*, tr. into French by Jean-Pierre Bagot (Paris: Cerf, 1985) p. 127. (Original: *Karl Rahner im Gespraech*, Munich, Koesel-Verlag, 1982.)
[51] *The Crucified God*, pp. 206, 231, 235.
[52] *Institutio*, p. 186.
[53] *Theological Investigations IV*, p. 113.

in himself can *himself* become subject to change *in something else*.[54] The 'power of subjecting himself to history', from which the power of creating derives, belongs, Rahner stresses, to his *love*, as God thus *expresses* himself faithfully.[55] Without subscribing to Rahner's kenoticism and idealistic anthropology, we may adopt his choice of words to tell of the supreme involvement of the unchangeable God, when the Word became flesh.

Conclusion

The biblical God only, as Heschel witnessed, is the Sovereign God: because he alone does not answer to extrapolations from the world, he alone is not born of idolatry. In Van Til's terms, he alone is non-correlative and autarcic: first and last, having life in himself and all fullness, needing no environment or partner to fulfill himself. The doctrine of the immanent or ontological Trinity, in its precedence over the trinitarian economy of creation and salvation, proclaims this truth indeed – the treasure of our faith. In this light, we recognize in the attempt to build the metaphysics of deity on events of history the loss both of our God's identity and of the concrete historical character of the Gospel (which breeds a poisonous universalism).

Precisely because God is the sovereign, non-correlative, self-sufficient and self-contained God above the universe, he is *free* to love. He is free to choose, and to visit, and to become, in hypostatic union without mixture or confusion, a man. He is no prisoner of the 'fixity'-pole in a world-derived dialectic of flux and changelessness. According to the same logic as we find in Exodus 19:5: 'You shall be a peculiar treasure unto me... *for* all the earth is mine', God is free to bind himself in Covenant with his created

---

[54] *Ibid.*
[55] *Ibid.*, p. 115.

partners *because* he has need of none and declares of himself *'anî-hû'*.

We cannot master this 'because'. The secret things belong to the Lord our God. But the things revealed belong to us and to our children for ever, so that we *can* sing:

Light of the world! for ever, ever shining,
There is no change in Thee!
True light of *life*, all joy and health enshrining,
Thou canst not fade nor flee.

DIVINE PASSIBILITY AND THE EARLY CHRISTIAN DOCTRINE OF GOD

PETER FORSTER

In the ascription of passion and passibility to the Godhead the lead in the present century has been taken by continental and overseas theologians, such as Bonhoeffer, Kitamori, and Moltmann. Yet, as historians of dogma are now beginning to acknowledge, this is an area in which English theology from the late nineteenth century anticipated later and wider developments. By the 1920's and 1930's efforts by earlier pioneers were the subject of mature reflection. At the behest of the Doctrine Commission of the Church of England, this period produced J.K. Mozley's excellent historical survey, *The Impassibility of God* (1926), and somewhat later O.C. Quick's discussion of the question of divine passibility in his widely read *Doctrines of the Creed*. Quick distinguishes three senses of the term passibility. Firstly, external passibility refers to the relations of one being towards another, that is the capacity to be acted upon from without − the capacity for passivity. Secondly, internal passibility refers to relations within a conscious being, wherein emotions and moods change, other than those under the control of their reason or will. In the third place there is sensational passibility, denoting the capacity to experience the sensations or feelings of pleasure and pain, in so far as a conscious subject is 'passive' in respect of these feelings or can be said to suffer them. The notion of sensational passibility refers in particular to the experience of pain or sorrow. We do not normally speak of 'suffering' pleasure or joy, and indeed the noun 'suffering' is often used as a synonym for 'pain'. In my broad survey of aspects of patristic theology relating to divine impassibility I will accept, in the background, Quick's distinctions. I begin by attempting to locate the apostolic doctrine of God in the experience of salvation.

So far as we are able to judge from the surviving documents, both canonical and extra-canonical, a sense of salvation dominated the life of the first generations of Christians.[1] It was from this sense of salvation that the belief arose that with Jesus Christ one had to do with God, the Creator and Lord of heaven and earth. Such intimations of the deity of Christ can be drawn from many different areas of the life and literature of emergent Christianity. As we look back upon this primitive and, we might almost say, natural sense of the divinity of Christ, we have to avoid two errors. The first, of which modern scholarship is only too aware, is to read back into this earliest period, the later enunciation of the doctrine of the Trinity, with its particular understanding of *homoousios*. But the second, of which modern scholarship is insufficiently aware, is to read back into this earliest period the Christological and Trinitarian doctrines of the period from the Apologists in the mid-second century to the early fourth century. If this is not explicitly done, by implication the same result is achieved when historians of doctrine simply ignore the literature of the first hundred years of Christianity. A good example of this failure to take proper account of Christian origins is provided by R.P.C. Hanson's recent *The Search for the Christian Doctrine of God* (T & T Clark, 1988) – a book which in many respects is most stimulating and illuminating.

Such authors, whose work evidences the debilitating division between biblical and systematic theology which is such a negative influence on both, tend to see the work of the Apologists, from Justin onwards, as a starting point for subsequent theology, rather than as a turning point in the witness and self-interpretation of early Christianity. This is to overlook the significance of the change of direction

---

[1] J. Pelikan provides a useful list in *The Christian Tradition*, vol. I, University of Chicago Press, 1971, p. 173.

which took place as the growing church consciously
encountered both the socio-political and the philosophical
culture of the Graeco-Roman world. A full consideration of
the emergence of the Apologists would be a digression,
but three related factors are of particular significance for
our theme.

The first is the tendency, beyond that which had gone
before, to seek an expression of Christian truth in the
philosophical idiom of the day. This formed one of the
classic themes of the early volumes of Harnack's great
History of Dogma, and it has been the subject of intensive
research throughout our century. Many of the key issues
are still widely debated; one thinks, for example, of the
philosophical influences on such different figures as Justin
and Arius, which are the subject of lively current debates.[2]
However, there can be little doubt that mainstream
Christianity took into its own expression a cluster of
aspects of the mature Greek conception of God, centred
around the essential otherness of God from the world. For
the mature Greek thought of the centuries immediately
prior to, and at the beginning of, the Christian era, taking
as our standard Platonism because this was the strongest
influence upon early Christian theology, God is the unified
origin of all things as they appear to us. From this followed
the conclusion that the ultimate origin of phenomena must
be quite distinct from and indeed antithetical to the
phenomenal world, viewed in its compound multiplicity and
transience.

The assimilation of God to a concept of supreme mind or
reason, allied to the dualism between body and soul,
reinforced this sense of divine otherness, and fed the

---

[2] For Justin, see, for example, R.M. Price, 'Hellenisation and the
Logos Doctrine in Justin', *Vigiliae Christianae, 42* (1987/88), pp. 18–
23. For Arius, see R.P.C. Hanson, *op.cit.*, and R.D. Williams, *Arius*,
D.L.T., 1987.

notion of the essential incomprehensibility of the divine, because for the Platonic tradition, owing to our corporeality, knowledge of purely intellectual realities is inevitably refracted and limited. This belief in the incomprehensibility of the divine grew in the Platonic tradition alongside the developing conception of the essential simplicity of God, with both reaching a final form in Neo-Platonism. Plotinus asserted that the ultimate One could not be understood as mind because mind is associated with a plurality of subject and object, the act of knowing and the object known.[3] If the full development of the idea of the simplicity of the ultimate origin of everything awaited Neo-Platonism, its essential features are already to be found in Plato: everything composite can also be divided, and consequently is mutable. Everything composite necessarily has a ground of its composition outside itself, and therefore cannot be the ultimate reality – a primitive version of the cosmological argument for the existence of God.

It is in this concept of God as the simple, self-existent ground of the universe that we see the basis for the characterisation of God as immutable. Closely related, we should note, is the concept of God as eternal, with eternity defined in strict opposition to time – an opposition which grew stronger as the Platonic tradition developed. In and with these features of the doctrine of God in the so-called 'cosmic religion' of the educated Graeco-Roman world, we meet the specific idea of the impassibility of God, and if we are to appreciate the implications of the idea of divine *apatheia* in the patristic age we have to see it as tied in with this range of aspects of God which set him dualistically aside from the realm of time, change, and becoming. This is a very different setting from that of the

---

[3] *Cf.* W. Pannenberg, 'The Appropriation of the Philosophical Concept of God as a Dogmatic Problem of Early Christian Theology', reprinted in *Basic Questions in Theology*, vol. II, SCM, 1971.

modern age, when the impassibility of God has been under
discussion, even if the differing backgrounds might be seen
as two opposing sides of the same coin. If the modern
discussion of the suffering of God has tended to assume
too anthropomorphic a concept of God, the ancient context
tended to assume that God could best be defined
antithetically from this-worldly reality.

There is, of course, a good deal of truth in the concept of
God as above and beyond 'the changes and chances of this
fleeting world'. As the Apologists sought to ward off
persecution, commend the Gospel to the educated second-
century Graeco-Roman world, and articulate the self-
understanding of the church, various influences led
towards the interaction with contemporary philosophy,
most notably in its Platonic or Middle-Platonic form. Was
it not Isaiah who had said of God: 'For my thoughts are
not your thoughts, neither are your ways my ways.... For
as the heavens are higher than the earth, so are my ways
higher than your ways and my thoughts than your
thoughts' (Is. 55:8f)? The 'otherness' of God was seen to
involve his immutability, however conceived, in such well-
known New Testament verses as James 1:17, 'Every good
endowment and every perfect gift is from above, coming
down from the Father of lights with whom there is no
variation or shadow of turning'. The God who is from
'everlasting to everlasting' was readily assimilated to a
Platonic eternity. It was relatively easy, then, for Justin to
refer in the language of philosophy to 'the unchangeable
and eternal God' (1 Apol. 13), and in the process the
biblical categories would acquire the overtones and
nuances of the philosophical account.

The Christian Apologists did not initiate this
rapprochement, which was there in the Septuagint, and
available in a sophisticated Jewish form in Philo. In general
terms, they are to be criticised neither for expressing
Christianity in the thought-forms of their day, nor for

linking Christian theology with the philosophical quest for universal truth. A proper conversation between theology and philosophy can only be of benefit to both disciplines. But they are separate disciplines, and this was insufficiently appreciated by the Apologists, and indeed by the Fathers in general. This inability sufficiently to distinguish the proper concerns of theology and philosophy inevitably led in the patristic age to a certain neglect of those features of the theological account of God which most deeply challenged the philosophical account: the particularity and historical character of revelation; indeed, revelation itself; the reality of incarnation; the essential freedom of the God of the Bible.

It has often been tempting in the history of doctrine to see revelation as in some ways supplementing the general or partial knowledge available through philosophical reasoning. The crucial difficulty with such a procedure is that philosophical theology does not readily leave gaps in its account to be filled from other sources; its account of the origin and source of all reality is intended to give as complete an account of that origin and source as possible. Therefore, if there is to be a serious engagement between philosophy and theology, it can only involve a complete and through-going transformation of the philosophy involved, even if the language and thought forms will doubtless to a degree survive in recognisable form. The first and general point I wish to make in relation to the Apologists is that their engagement with contemporary philosophy did not reach this transformative depth. Put in terms of our present theme, the philosophical notion of divine impassibility, for all its coherence with certain features of both Old and New Testaments, did not engage sufficiently with other aspects of the God of the Bible, notably but by no means exclusively the story of the crucifixion. Ignatius' 'passion of my God', it might provocatively and provisionally be suggested, became largely still-born. The best way of further investigating

how and why this came to pass will be to move to the
second key aspect of the Apologists' theology, its
hierarchical view of both the Godhead and its relation to
creation.

Although the central concern of the New Testament is
the redemption of the world through Jesus Christ, the motif
of creation is not absent, and in the New Testament itself
we see forged the basic link between incarnation and
creation, wherein Christ is seen as the agent or mediator
of creation. It was a relatively small step to conceive
Christ's role within the hierarchical scheme offered by
second-century Middle-Platonism. The precise extent of
the dependence of Justin upon Middle-Platonism has
recently been challenged, but a certain dependence seems
undeniable.[4] In Middle-Platonism the world-soul of Plato
had developed into an inferior, secondary deity who
mediated between the First God and the world. In effect,
as a stronger sense of one first principle developed in the
Platonic tradition, doubtless in part influenced by
Aristotle's unmoved First Mover, this exacerbated the
inherent dualism of the system. The Middle-Platonic
scheme has to be seen, therefore, as something of a Trojan
Horse within second-century theology: outwardly
attractive in the light of the aims and interests of the
Apologetic movement, but in danger of offering a false
legitimacy for a dualistic outlook. In Justin we see Christ
interpreted primarily as the *Logos* of God, with the concept
of *Logos* further interpreted against a background of Stoic
and Platonic terms, with Stoic monism to a degree
softening Platonic dualism.[5] For the Stoics the concept of

---

[4] The challenge is from R.M. Price, *op.cit.*. The earlier account by
R.A. Norris, *God and the World in Early Christian Theology*, is
more reliable.

[5] Superficially, Justin's use of the *Logos* concept suggests a
dependence upon the Fourth Gospel. In fact, as scholars have long
recognised, at best it is uncertain whether he had any acquaintance
with it.

Peter R. Forster

rational *Logos* denoted the cosmic spirit whose operation held the world together, and for the Platonists the world-soul mediates between the First God and the world. The identification between Christ and the *Logos* and the Platonic world-soul was given superficial support by the idea that Plato had cribbed some of his ideas from Moses. This theory drew its inner strength from the common conviction that the older an idea was the more likely it was to be true, in effect a theory of epistemological immutability, which reflects the ontological immutability in Greek thought. The identification of Christ the *Logos* with a philosophically conceived mediator was further bolstered by the existing rapprochement between the Platonic notion of the world-soul and the Word or Wisdom of God as conceived in late Judaism.

From this we can see the background to the particular form taken by the *Logos* doctrine in the Apologists. Although we see a development from Justin to Tatian, Theophilus and Tertullian, the pattern is clearly established.[6] Before creation, the supreme God brought forth from within himself his Word, as his rational expression, to be both the agent or instrument of creation and the means by which he would relate to creation. In fact, the stress is on the second function, and in the Apologists there are only relatively sparse references to the *Logos* as the agent of creation.[7] Creation tends to be attributed to the supreme God alone, as the decision to create takes precedence over the decision to generate – or bring forth – the *Logos*. In effect, the second-century *Logos*

---

[6] For the development of the *Logos* doctrine in the Apologists, see A.I.C. Heron, '"Logos, Image, Son": Some Models and Paradigms in Early Christology', in *Creation, Christ and Culture: Studies in Honour of T.F. Torrance*, ed. R.W.A. McKinney, T. & T. Clark, pp. 43–62.

[7] The textbooks are widely misleading on this point. To take the case of Justin, with but few exceptions (*1 Apol.* 59 (?), 64; *2 Apol.* 6) he attributes creation entirely to the transcendent 'Father of all'.

theology is an uneasy compromise between monotheistic monarchy and Trinitarian theology, with the mediational *Logos* both reduced in status and role in comparison with the Nicene doctrine, and also usurping the role of the Spirit, for whom in the second-century theology of the Apologists there is little place. This is not to deny the limited usefulness and validity of the Apologists' *Logos* theology. It helpfully avoided mythological interpretations of Christ as 'Son of God', and provided a readily understandable basis for the universal claims of the Gospel. But the problems remain, and take two particular forms.

Firstly, Christ as the *Logos* of God tends to be seen as part of a descending chain of being, taking central stage in the communication of the knowledge and power of God to the world. Formally this would seem potentially Arian in structure, and this type of thinking undoubtedly contributed to Arianism; but fundamentally it should be seen as anti-Arian. Justin and the other Apologists would not have placed the line between God and creation between Father and the *Logos*/Son, but below the *Logos*/Son (and Spirit?). It was on precisely this ground that Marcellus of Anyra, whose theology of the *Logos* bears striking resemblance to that of the second century, made a strong attack on Arianism in the early fourth century. As one reads Justin's defence of his theology, it is clear that he wants the *Logos*/Son in some sense to share the divinity of the Father, as God from God, fire from fire, light from the sun. Yet this derivation or generation from the ingenerate Father leads him to conceive the *Logos* as, in some sense, an inferior sort of 'second God', assimilated to the Platonic world-soul. The result is a certain compromise between Christianity and Platonism, with the second person of the Trinity associated with both the ingenerate and immutable realm of Being, and the more dubious realm of becoming. If this is true in the very generation or sending forth of the *Logos*, in his theophanic appearances in Old Testament times and in the presence of the *Logos spermatikos* to the pagan world, it is particularly true in the incarnation. In a recent study it has been shown that for Justin the theophanic and inspirational activity of the *Logos* are best seen as prefigurements of the incarnation, with the incarnation itself interpreted in terms of a Christology of humiliation/exaltation.[8] Trakatellis has demonstrated how the great expansion of the language of pre-existence in Justin served to undergird the understanding of the incarnation as the humiliation of Christ in the flesh, prior to his exaltation, or, we might say, re-exaltation in the resurrection and ascension. Is the scene set for a theology of the suffering *Logos*/Son, who, by his mediational link with the supreme Father offers an anticipation of the modern conception of a suffering God?

If in a sense the scene is set, we must say that the play did not begin, even if some of the parts were rehearsed. Even if, on the basis of the New Testament, a theology of a suffering Godhead were permissible, it does not develop in Justin. He is a teacher who attempts to carry forward the traditions of the apostolic age, and these include both a high place for the cross and resurrection, and a belief in the soteriological importance of the passion of Christ. But the many references in Justin to the cross and resurrection do not really extend beyond the level of mere statement. He neither explicates nor really defends the saving significance of the cross, and his chief purpose is to show that the series of principal events concerning Christ were foretold by Scripture, a variation on the 'oldest is best' theme. His chief defence of the cross, interestingly, is to interpret it symbolically as power and triumph, a cross-like shape being visible in the masts of ships, the structure of military banners, and the erect arms-outstretched form

---

[8] D.C. Trakatellis, *The Pre-existence of Christ in Justin Martyr*, Harvard: Scholars Press, 1976.

of the body of an adult man.[9] We are here some way from
Paul, for whom the cross was foolishness for the Gentiles,
and the power and wisdom of God only for the called. Nor
do we glimpse the irony of the Gospel of John, when that
Gospel speaks of the cross as exaltation. Indeed, far from
Justin's scheme offering a concept of a passible, suffering
God, it might be said that it is designed precisely to
protect the ingenerate, immutable, eternal Father from
unseemly contact with his mutable creation. The only
qualification which should be offered to such a judgment is
that it is easy to underestimate the extent to which an
author like Justin had in fact embraced primitive Christian
tradition — and, at Rome, not least the tradition handed on
by Paul.

The second fundamental problem with the hierarchical
Logos theology also bears closely on our theme. In
avoiding the problem of Arianism, this theology inevitably
faced the problem of preserving the integrity and
unchangeability of God through the primal act of the
generation of the *Logos*. This is approached in various
ways, for example by recourse to the underlying ambiguity
of the meaning of *Logos* as both reason and spoken word,
to which was appended the Stoic distinction between the
logos endiathetos and *logos prophorikos*. Tatian and
Tertullian (who was probably dependent on Tatian at this
point) also try to emphasise the continuity between
Father and *Logos* by the notion of the 'power of the *logos*'
inherent in the Father. In the process there is some
softening of Justin's idea of Christ as 'a second God', but
the greater sophistication in the accounts of the later
Apologists does not really solve the inherent problem of
the apparent divisibility and changeability of God.[10]

---

[9] See especially, *1 Apol.* 55. He clearly has in mind in particular the
figure of the Emperor.
[10] *Cf.* A.I.C. Heron, *op. cit.*

Although Irenaeus engaged in an important modification of Justin's theology, it was left to Origen, with his acute awareness of the educated pagan critique of Christianity, to meet head-on the problem of the generation of the Son compromising the ingeneracy and immutability of the Father. He did this by using the Christological motifs of sonship and image as his basis for the concept of the eternal generation of the Son. The notion of Christ as *Logos* is almost relegated to describe a particular function carried out by the eternal Son, who is the image of the Father. The dogmatic elucidation of the concept of the eternal sonship of Christ was a permanent gain for Christian tradition. However, because Origen, for all his undoubted greatness, failed to carry through a radical Christian critique of Platonism, meeting one of the problems of the Apologists' theology merely served to exacerbate the other: the problem of hierarchy in God, and in God's relation to the world. The temporal subordination of the *Logos* in the Apologists becomes for Origen an eternal subordination, even if, with the second-century Apologists, the Son is regarded, in some way, as essentially divine.

One can readily see why Origen has sometimes been regarded as the father alike of Arianism and Nicene orthodoxy. In the *Contra Celsum* there is no dispute between Origen and Celsus over the unchangeability of God.[11] Indeed, the agreement over Platonic tenets is much wider: God is incorporeal, and quite separate from corruptible matter. The soul is superior to the body, and the image of God in man resides in the soul and not in the body.[12] Any attribution of human passion to God is thus

---

[11] Many scholars have held that Celsus' critique of Christianity was aimed primarily at Justin, and Origen in effect purges Justin's theology of any suggestion that God is mutable.

[12] Origen thus opposes the earlier Christian tradition, manifest most clearly in Irenaeus, that the image resides in body and soul together.

rejected as inherently unworthy or impious. Faced with the
apparent biblical ascription of human passion to God,
Origen has recourse to three arguments. Firstly, the
language of the Bible, especially when it speaks of wrath
or anger in God, is not 'the finest language possible', but
the result of God speaking down or accommodating himself
to us, as stern parents are wont to speak to errant
children. Secondly, texts which appear to attribute human
passion to God need to be interpreted in the light of other
texts which eschew such thoughts.[13] Thirdly, and, for our
purposes probably of greatest interest, Origen offers
certain theological points to guide the intelligent
interpreter of difficult passages. Central to these is the
doctrine of the two advents of Christ, the first in
humiliation and the second in glory, where he develops
ideas found earlier in Justin. This enables Origen both to
claim Isaiah 53 and analogous texts as prophecy of Christ,
while preserving God from human passion:

> Celsus... and all who have not believed in Jesus, have
> failed to notice that the prophecies speak of two
> advents of Christ. In the first he is subject to human
> passions and deeper humiliation, in order that by being
> with men Christ might teach the way that leads to God,
> and might leave no-one living this life among men an
> opportunity of defending themselves on the grounds
> that they were ignorant of the judgment to come. In the
> second he is coming in glory and in divinity alone,
> without any human passions bound up with his divine
> nature.[14]

In the New Testament there is a certain distinction
between the two comings – or appearings – of Christ, but
this distinction is within the over-arching and integrating
concept of the *parousia*. The passion is enacted in the

---

[13] *Contra Celsum*, IV. 71ff.
[14] *Contra Celsum*, I. 56.

'first' coming, but the Lamb who sits on the throne is to be seen as slain before the foundation of the world, and the Lord for whose coming the church prays still bears the marks of the cross. In the Platonic tradition in the early church, from Justin to Origen, we see the passion and all that relates to it confined with rigour to the first coming in the flesh, and in the process we see a certain hardening in the belief in the essential unchangeability of God.

It is in this context of the temporary humiliation of Christ in his first coming that we will best understand the short treatise of Origen's pupil, Gregory Thaumaturgos, *On the Impassibility of God*. First and foremost a pastor and preacher, Gregory doubtless had to wrestle in a particular way with the role of suffering and crucifixion in relation to God. His basic conclusion was that since God was free to decide to come in humiliation in his first coming in order to come in glory in his second, he is free to suffer in order to defeat death. What matters to Gregory is that any apparent and temporary suffering is a mere episode in God's victorious activity, and therefore cannot in any sense be construed as divine weakness. In his essence God remained impassible in suffering, unchangeable like a blacksmith's anvil when assailed by iron and fire. Inasmuch as Gregory does not have recourse to the notion that all suffering in Christ must be attributed to his humanity alone, his instinct was sound, but the elevation of will over nature in God, an elevation which his master Origen had been unwilling to countenance, was to come to a sticky end at Athanasius' hands.[15] Gregory is left asserting that God suffers without suffering, which, if interpreted by Quick's distinctions, may be a formulation which points in the right direction, but for Gregory the

---

[15] Recourse to a sharp distinction between essence and will would not readily elicit the sympathy of later Platonism or Christian Platonism. See the discussion, with relation to Plotinus and Augustine, by H. Chadwick, 'Freedom and Necessity in Early Christian Thought about God', in *Concilium, 166* (1983).

constancy and freedom of the God of the Bible has not
escaped the philosophically-inspired conceptuality of
immutability and impassibility.

These developments in the Alexandrian tradition with
Origen and his successors helped to prepare the ground for
the Trinitarian and Christological disputes over the divinity
of Christ and the nature of the incarnation, with which the
church in the succeeding two centuries was to struggle.
But if we are to understand the bearing of notions of divine
impassibility upon the fourth and fifth-century debates, we
need to return to the third basic factor in the development
of theology in the second century. This is the precedence of
cosmological over soteriological concerns.

In asserting this precedence we have to proceed with
caution. In the martyr centuries a sense of the reality of
salvation in Christ doubtless extended far beyond that
indicated in the literary deposit from educated Christians
through which we now have largely to view the Early
Church. We noted earlier that there is strong evidence of
this sense of salvation in the evidence relating to the first
hundred years or so of the church. This is taken forward in
the succeeding generation, but it is not fully taken up by
them. We noted this in the case of Justin, and the
quotation just adduced from Origen presents in a particular
form an exemplarist view of the atonement: Christ has
come in the flesh to 'teach the way that leads to God and
to leave no-one living this life among men an opportunity
of defending themselves on the ground that they were
ignorant of the judgment to come'. Along with the schema
of the two advents of Christ has emerged a schema of two
rather disconnected judgments, the weight being placed
firmly on the judgment to come, which is interpreted in
individualistic terms. Each person has been placed under
certain philosophically specifiable conditions with freedom
to do right or wrong, judgment being pronounced by God
beyond death.

This is a bit of a caricature of authors like Justin and Origen, but it enshrines important elements of their theology. Different writers will conceive in somewhat different ways the role of the historical revelation in Christ in altering the scales of justice, but the strong moralistic strand especially in the more philosophically influenced writers in the Early Church is widespread. Merging with certain strands in the Latin tradition, it reached both its zenith and its *denouement* in Pelagius, who found ample witness to his views in earlier writers. It operates with a view of God as, at the end of the day, little more than a cosmic regulator, charged with creating a world in which good can be achieved and justice is fair. Such a God may well have intervened in Christ to draw a line under past sins and offer a fresh start, and this wiping clean of the slate may even, as in the case of Pelagius, utilise something like a concept of penal substitution, but God's present role is still limited, in effect, to the cosmological rather than the soteriological. To put this slightly differently, salvation is the product of the operation of a cosmic system which includes God at its head – a typically philosophical overall conception.

The manner in which soteriology was subordinated to cosmology can be illustrated in three ways which bear directly on our overall theme: the patristic approach to salvation, to providence, and to Christology.

In relation to the approach to salvation in the Early Church reference has already been made to the 'exemplarist' understanding of the atonement in Origen, who here builds upon Clement and, to a degree, the earlier Apologists and Apostolic Fathers. Such a 'subjective' view does not stand alone, but the objective conceptions of atonement which we find in the Fathers bear the clear marks of a hierarchical, cosmic framework. This is especially true of the idea of deification or divinisation

38

which came to assume such an important place in the
concept of salvation. The notion of 'participation in the
divine nature' is, of course, found in the New Testament,
although in a context which is firmly Christological and
ethical. The range of meaning given to the term deification
in patristic thought has been usefully discussed by H.E.W.
Turner in *The Patristic Doctrine of Redemption*. Amid
considerable variety, a basic trend emerges wherein the
early use of the idea develops out of a mainly
eschatological and Christological key into one which is
progressively physical and mystical, Origen again being an
important figure. To quote Professor Turner:

> Origen thinks almost of a hierarchy of Being formed by
> God himself, the Logos of God and those who through
> the Logos of God have begun to receive their deification
> through the Logos. For such a deification of man to be
> possible there must still remain after the Fall a certain
> natural affinity between God and man.[16]

Turner makes three overall points about this tradition.
Firstly, although the outlines are present in Ignatius and
Irenaeus, the hesitations of these earlier writers lest the
idea verge in a gnostic direction are largely swept aside.
Secondly, there is a marked difference between the early
notions which associate divinisation firmly with the
incarnate Christ, as our lives are recapitulated in his, and
the later view, with roots in the Greek Apologists, which
conceives of the redemptive action of the *Logos* in apparent
independence of the incarnation. Thirdly, the concept of
divinisation made an important contribution to the rise of
Eutychianism and the Monophysite tradition. This
development of the notion of divinisation both reposes
upon and reinforces the understanding of the impassibility
of God which we discussed earlier. This is explicit in
Justin: if Christians keep the commandments, they become

---

[16] *Op. cit.*, p. 80.

like God, impassible and immortal,[17] and it probably lies behind Ignatius' description of the eucharist as the medicine of immortality.[18] The correlation between Christian and divine *apatheia* develops in the Christian Platonic tradition, partly under Stoic influence. While Clement of Alexandria draws a distinction between divine and human *apatheia*, Origen comes close to identifying them, as Philo before him had done.[19] As so often is the case in theology, a false dualism, in this case that inherent in the hierarchic cosmology too readily embraced in the Early Church, tends to encourage a counterbalancing monism of soul and the divine, aided here by the developing contrast between body and soul.

It might be suggested that the divinisation theory, taken to an extreme, is the equivalent, or inverse, myth in the Early Church corresponding to the more radical modern accounts of a passible God. In each case there is a false approximation of divine and human reality, starting from opposite sides. Another rather mythological strand of the patristic understanding of redemption, perhaps closer in nature to the myth of a suffering God when this concept becomes too anthropomorphic, is provided by the theory of a ransom paid to the devil. In its own way, this theory can also be related to the underlying conception of a God imprisoned in his own immutability: God as the rich man arranged for an intermediary to pay the necessary ransom, while he stays at a safe distance, higher up the hierarchy of being. Substitute 'penalty' for 'ransom' and you are not far from unsatisfactory aspects of some concepts of penal

---

[17] *Dialogue*, 124.4 cf. *2 Apol.* 1.2.

[18] Ignatius explicitly describes the divine nature in Christ as impassible (*Eph.* 7.2; *Polyc.* 3.2), whereas the New Testament does not use the term.

[19] See R.M. Grant, *The Early Christian Doctrine of God*, University of Virginia Press, 1966, p. 112ff.

substitution. In each case we meet an anthropomorphic projection onto God of certain notions of 'justice'.[20]

A brief consideration of the patristic understanding of providence provides a second illustration of the problematic consequences of giving precedence to cosmology over soteriology. This relates in particular to divine passibility in the first of Quick's senses: the capacity to be acted on. There is unanimity among the Fathers that God is in control of his world, and that events that occur in the world correspond to his mysterious counsel and foreknowledge. This does not entail the belief that everything occurs as a result of his direct volition, and distinctions are commonly made between different forms of the divine will, as directive or permissive, but all ultimately falls within a 'grand design'. Such assertions recur throughout the early centuries and, as J.N.D. Kelly has demonstrated in detail, the confession of God as 'Father almighty' was one of the first and basic components of the creeds of the Early Church.[21] God's providential ordering of the universe was commonly seen to provide an important argument for his existence and goodness.

It was at this point that the Early Church was probably most influenced by Stoic ideas, for the Stoics were strong

---

[20] In the patristic case of the rationale of the theory of ransom to the devil, see Gregory of Nyssa, *Great Catechism*, 20f. It is outside the scope of this paper to pursue the interesting question of how far the restatement of the idea of penal substitution in recent evangelical writing implies a significant amendment to traditional views of divine impassibility. When, for example, John Stott speaks of 'divine self-satisfaction through divine self-substitution' (*The Cross of Christ*, IVP, 1986, the essential argument of which is usefully summarised in *Essentials*, D.L. Edwards and J. Stott, Hodder & Stoughton, 1988, pp. 158–168), it would be useful to know what alteration to the traditional concept of divine impassibility is envisaged.

[21] *Early Christian Creeds*, 3rd edit., Longmans, 1972, pp. 131–139.

defenders of a providence wherein all is arranged by God for the best. Although the Church rejected the fatalism and immanentism inherent in the Stoic scheme, it did not properly integrate its belief in freedom with its belief in providence.[22] Too readily, fatalism was merely replaced by the foreknowledge of all things by a timeless God. The belief in the freedom of man was then easily truncated to a notion of power-over-oneself, *autexousia*, which was required to allow God to exercise a just judgment on human affairs.[23] There is little or no sense that in creating a reality distinct from himself, a reality which has within it self-conscious man, God put himself, to use the modern parlance, 'at risk'. Yet the story of the incarnation, with its climax on the cross, does seem to point to a doctrine of divine vulnerability, at least in some form, and this the Fathers, with their particular doctrine of divine impassibility, were scarcely able to countenance.

There are large questions here, which require to be taken up more systematically elsewhere. Is God ultimately subject to frustration by human activity? What are the proper limits of a concept of divine vulnerability, both on the cross and, as the cross is reflected throughout history, when the purposive love of God encounters resistance and frustration? To suggest that the God disclosed in the incarnation is vulnerable to the choices exercised by his creation does not necessarily imply that God is inherently weak. The converse could be asserted: vulnerability is freely accepted by God in the act and consequence of creation precisely because, as the God who is capable of the novelty of creation, he is infinitely

---

[22] I have sought to demonstrate this in relation to Irenaeus in my as yet unpublished doctoral thesis, *God and the World in St Irenaeus*, University of Edinburgh, 1985.

[23] It is a little noticed fact that the frequently repeated patristic attribution to man of *autexousia* has no New Testament precedent, where the concept of *eleutheria* might better be translated in modern idiom as 'liberation' rather than as 'freedom'.

equipped to meet the challenge posed by the freedom and
spontaneity of creation. That is to say, rather than speak
with the Fathers simply of *the* plan of God for his world,
we need to recognise the infinite number of sub-plans
which God will employ to secure a satisfactory fulfilment of
his overall plan.[24] It is significant that there is reluctance
among the Fathers to speak of God as infinite, because of
the Greek association between infinity and irrationality.
Although the patristic authors could conceive God as
essentially 'rich',[25] they did not explicate this richness in
terms of resourcefulness and adaptability, because of the
underlying axiom of unchangeability, and the doctrine of
providence inevitably drifted in a static direction, preparing
the way, perhaps, for the Augustinian doctrine of
predestination.

In these three related ways, its use of philosophical
theology, its utilisation of a hierarchical ontology, and its
precedence of cosmology over soteriology, the theology of
the Apologists bequeathed difficulties to patristic
theology, and in each case we meet the rather uncritical
adoption of the axiom of divine impassibility.

The next area of patristic theology to merit discussion is
Christology. The Arian controversy used to be regarded as
the instance in the Early Church *par excellence* when
philosophical and cosmological considerations swamped
the specifically Christian conception of salvation. Recent
years have seen efforts to defend the soteriological
character of especially early Arianism, notably through the
book by Gregg and Groh, *Early Arianism: A View of
Salvation* (SCM, 1981). The particular argument advanced

---

[24] I have in mind the interesting suggestions offered by J.R. Lucas,
Freedom and Grace, SPCK, 1976, which have recently been taken up
by other writers on creation and providence, for example V.
Brummer, *What Are We Doing When We Pray?*, SCM, 1984, and J.
Polkinghorne, *Science and Providence*, SPCK, 1989.
[25] This is a particular attribute of God in Irenaeus.

here has been strongly criticised, and it is more helpful for us to approach the issue through R.P.C. Hanson's treatment of fourth-century trinitarian theology, *The Search for the Christian Doctrine of God*, where he partly accepts yet radically revises the proposals made by Gregg and Groh. For our purpose, Hanson concludes that for early Arianism soteriology and cosmology are closely linked, and he summarises his discussion of the basic rationale of Arianism as follows:

> At the heart of the Arian Gospel was a God who suffered. Their elaborate theology of the relation of the Son to the Father, which so much preoccupied their opponents, was devised in order to find a way of envisaging a Christian doctrine of God which would make it possible to be faithful to the Biblical witness to a God who suffers. This was to be achieved by conceiving of a lesser God as reduced divinity who would be ontologically capable, as the High God was not, of enduring human experiences, including suffering and death. This might be called an exemplarist soteriology, not in the sense that they presented the example of a man gaining perfection by moral effort, but in the sense that it was an example of God suffering as man suffers, or at least what man suffers, in order to redeem man.[26]

Despite the obvious and welcome gain in our understanding of Arianism which has been achieved in recent years, the concept of Christ as a reduced divinity whose suffering enables the impassibility of the supreme God to remain intact looks as unsatisfactory as ever. It is not even clear, on Hanson's account, just why the suffering of the reduced divinity results in our salvation: his final claim, that the suffering of Christ was 'in order to redeem man' simply hangs in the air, without any

---

[26] *Op. cit.*, p. 121.

supporting explanation. Any reference to suffering in relation to atonement, whether the subject of the suffering be God the Father, God the Son, or the humanity of Christ alone, has to offer some explanation of the connection between suffering and atonement. Hanson rightly rejects the exemplarist account given by Gregg and Groh, but it is quite unclear what he would suggest in its place. For all their apparent promise for our theme, these recent developments in Arian scholarship may be passed over relatively quickly, in favour of a consideration of some aspects of the patristic account of the person of Christ.

The Arians shared with the later Apollinarians the belief that Christ had a human body but that the divine *Logos* stood in place of the human soul. The Arians held that the Nicene two-nature doctrine struck at the heart of the doctrine of salvation, because a mere man could not be the appointed Saviour of mankind. For those holding the Nicene position, and thus barred the Arian route to the accommodation of God to suffering, the question of the impassibility of God was posed in a particular way, which intensified once the *homoousios* gained widespread acceptance. The Apollinarian approach was based, in effect, upon an extension of the divinisation theory, examined earlier. For them it was only because the *Logos* was immutable and impassible that the fallibility and passibility of humanity is overcome and salvation obtained. Apollinaris assumed that every mind was a self-moving, self-governing will, and that therefore two such entities could not exist in one person, especially if one were changeable and the other unchangeable.[27] The Apollinarian position represents one development of the early Athanasian perception that salvation depends upon God remaining immutable in order to free man from his sin and mortality. Hence the seemingly endless scholarly saga

---

[27] There is a good discussion of these points in F. Young, *From Nicea to Chalcedon*, SCM, 1983, pp. 184ff.

of Athanasius' relation to Apollinarianism. As mature two-nature Christology crystallised out of Nicene theology, the overall philosophical context, with its ingrained hierarchical modes of thought, ensured that the problem of the apparent co-existence in one person of two 'natures', or centres of consciousness, became central. The axiom of impassibility as applied to the essential nature of God tended to slant the problem in a particular way, and the modern interest in divine impassibility has ensured that recent surveys of the period have paid full attention to this dimension.[28] The most marked effect was in Antiochene Christology, with its resistance to the Alexandrian assertion that Mary should be the bearer of the whole Christ, as *theotokos*. The emphasis upon the historical Jesus in the Antiochene tradition, when confronted with the philosophically-influenced concept of God, led the theologians of that tradition towards a rather dualist separation between the divine and human natures of Christ. The apparently awkward gospel tradition of a suffering Christ was easily accommodated in Antiochene theology, as had been the case earlier with Tertullian, by the attribution of suffering solely to the human nature, as a distinct reality in itself. Such attribution would then serve to harden the underlying dualism. Despite the undeniable subtlety and variety in the Antiochene tradition, the charge that the axiom of impassibility drew this theology towards a division in the person of Christ seems justifiable.

The situation in the Alexandrian tradition, as exemplified by Cyril, is more interesting for our theme. His basic affirmations are set out in his *Second Letter to Nestorius*, wherein, after asserting that the Word

---

[28] In addition to the important works by Young and Hanson already cited, mention should be made of Elert's influential study, *Der Ausgang der altchristlichen Christologie*, Berlin, Lutherisches Verlagshaus, 1957. Elert's work on fourth and fifth-century Christology is integrated with a good modern discussion in C. Gunton, *Yesterday and Today*, DLT, 1983.

remained the subject in Christ after the incarnation, the
assumption of humanity being 'in a manner mysterious and
inconceivable', he continues:

> We do not mean that God the Word suffered blows,
> nail-piercings or other wounds in his own nature, since
> the divine is impassible because it is incorporeal, but
> what is said is that since his own created body suffered
> these things he himself is said to have suffered for our
> sake, the point being that within the suffering body was
> the Impassible.[29]

Cyril thus acknowledges the Antiochene insistence upon
the divine immutability, but equally wishes to make the
eternal Son the subject of the incarnation and all that went
with it. His way of holding both poles together is to
distance the impassible *Logos* from the sufferings which
were consequent upon the assumption of human flesh, yet
to assert that all the experiences of Christ are in a sense
reckoned or attributed to the divine Logos, by virtue of the
process of incarnation. In defending his position he often
emphasises the inconceivability and mystery of the
hypostatic union, and he also makes a significant appeal to
the union of divine and created reality in the eucharist.
There we receive 'the personal, truly life-giving flesh of
God the Word himself'.[30] But, fundamentally, he is trying
to interpret the Gospel story of the incarnation as a story
with God incarnate as the subject. Hence his frequent
appeal to Philippians 2. His difficulties arise because he is
obliged to express himself in the rather physical, static
categories of his day, even if he is patently attempting to
transcend them. This attempt is most evident when he
tries to explain the *kenosis* of the Son of God, to which
Paul had given witness. For Cyril, *kenosis* means that the

---

[29] *Second Letter to Nestorius*, 5. The translation is taken from the
edition, with text, in the *O.E.C.T.* series, ed. L.R. Wickham.
[30] *Third Letter to Nestorius*, 8.

Word, 'abased himself by submitting to the limitations of the human condition'.[31] In the incarnation, then, the Word enters upon conditions of existence 'inferior' to those which belong to him as he is in himself, and this not so much as a new state of affairs resulting from a composition or mixing of two natures, but rather as a history of the *Logos*, and therefore a history of God. Compared with his great predecessor and mentor, Athanasius, it is a thorough-going inclusion of the fullness of manhood in Christ, exemplified by his unwillingness to attribute the more 'human' dimension of the New Testament account of Jesus to his humanity alone, which enables Cyril somewhat to transcend the limits set by the rather static divinisation motif of salvation through union with God. Of course, the modern expression 'a history of God' is quite anachronistic if applied to Cyril, whose ultimate acceptance of the axiom of divine immutability is effectively unqualified, but among the Fathers it is perhaps his thought which, despite still lacking a proper correlation between Christology and the atonement, points most clearly in the direction of modern developments. His Christology has often been accused of muddle and confusion, and to a cursory view this judgment seems justified, but it is better to see this unevenness and ambiguity as resulting from his attempt to express a form of kenotic Christology in thoughtforms which were hardly up to the task, and which, especially with the axiom of immutability, were a hindrance.

Cyril's Christology bears a certain relation to that of Irenaeus in the second century. Irenaeus distanced himself from the *Logos* theology of the Apologists, which must have seemed akin to the emanationist and changing

---

[31] From *Quod Unus Sit Christus*, quoted in R.A. Norris, 'Christological Models in Cyril of Alexandria', *Studia Patristica, 13* (1975), p. 259. This article provides an excellent guide to Cyril's Christology.

Gnostic Godhead, and he anticipated Origen's formulation of the eternal generation of the Son. Lacking the subordinationism in Origen or the Apologists, he associates Christ very closely with the Father, but more than any other of the Fathers he also maintains a strong emphasis on the humanity of Christ. Against the Gnostic division between Christ and Jesus, he repeatedly stresses the unity of the person of the one Jesus Christ,[32] and on this basis develops the soteriological motif of recapitulation. The ingredients are here for the type of reflection we see in Cyril, but the prominent and particular role of suffering in the Gnostic godhead, and its limited and, to Irenaeus' eyes, weak nature, helped to steer him in the direction which subsequent theology took. The word is quiescent, as the humanity of Christ suffers.[33] The doctrine of recapitulation, for all its undoubted merits, loses something of the agony, the cutting edge, of the Pauline theology from whence it had been quarried, and it acquires the rather rational and physical character we saw in the subsequent divinisation theme. Irenaeus' theology comes out of the Asia Minor traditions which included the Ignatian 'passion of my God', but this aspect of Ignatius is not taken up. The close – and proper – association between Christ and God remains, and in the absence of the full New Testament soteriology indeed tends to become too close.

We see this in particular in the so-called patripassionism consequent upon the modalism, also with roots in Asia Minor, which Tertullian countered. For all that there may be an element of truth in the tenets of patripassionism, because it drew a firm distinction between nature and will in God, and attributed suffering only to the divine will, it could not approach the ground covered in modern discussions of the concept of a crucified

---

[32] This is *the* theme of *Adversus Haereses*, Book III.
[33] *Adversus Haereses*, III. 19.3.

Peter

Peter R. Forster

God. The modalist controversy is really an early Trinitarian controversy, rather than a controversy over the impassibility of God, and third-century modalism was not an attempt to challenge the concept of the *apatheia* of the divine essence. Inasmuch as it was portrayed as doing so, 'patripassionism' tended to harden the concept of impassibility held by its opponents, and to encourage the ascription of the 'human' features of Jesus to his humanity alone, a process well illustrated in Tertullian.

In conclusion let me briefly review the relation of this broad sway of patristic theology to the different aspects of impassibility distinguished by Quick. Firstly, with regard to external passibility, the capacity to be acted on from without, with but the partial exception of the Christology of Cyril of Alexandria, there is little to be said. It is here that the inner conflict between the Platonic doctrine of God, and the Christian tradition of incarnational theology, was at its sharpest. If one is tempted to say that Platonism won on points, it would perhaps be fairer to speak of a draw, and a rematch in later centuries when the rules had been changed! Secondly, with regard to internal and sensational passibility, Christian theology shared with high philosophical theology a horror of the Homeric or Gnostic myths. Although this did not result in any formal denial of the essential personhood of God, we can perhaps identify a certain attenuation, especially in the Western tradition. Does much modern theology encompass an over-reaction, wherein an idealist projection of personality into God, well evidenced in notions of a social Trinity, underlies the new myth of a suffering God? This may help us to understand why notions of a suffering Godhead and a social Trinity have been distinctively, although by no means exclusively, Anglican themes. This essay has sought to demonstrate that the key to an answer must lie in the doctrine of atonement, the point where patristic theology is probably at its weakest. The emphasis in the Fathers upon atonement as the overcoming of death is correct, but the

50

manner in which this insight is expounded is unsatisfactory. The early emphasis upon Christianity as a way – the way – of salvation was, so far as the chief theological debates of the time were concerned, to a significant degree obscured. The role of the axiom of impassibility in this process is undeniable.

GOD AND CHANGE : MOLTMANN IN THE LIGHT OF THE REFORMED TRADITION

PAUL WELLS

Several difficulties beset presenting such a vast subject in synoptic form. Problems of selection and objectivity arise in due course, but perhaps the greatest obstacle concerns natural prejudices which determine our attitudes in many instances where comparisons are used. Classical theism may seem essentially unattractive, whereas Moltmann's recent contributions are impressively stimulating and seem relevant to the dialogue between Christianity and modern culture.

Two initial considerations
1. *A shift in theological accentuation*
Moltmann's comments on the question of change in God can be considered in the light of increasing criticism of classical theism over the last half-century. This is documented in a profusion of sources.[1] In the past the impassibility of God was self-evident; the concepts of God and change were taken to be incompatible. Today it is not uncommon to read affirmations such as: 'the concept of divine suffering is not only the core of our faith but the uniqueness of Christianity.'[2] Even in evangelical circles, Clark Pinnock has called for a re-evaluation of divine

---

[1] One only has to look through the *Scottish Journal of Theology*. See, in particular, T. R. Pollard, 'The impassibility of God', 8 (1955) 353-364, K. J. Woollcombe, 'The Pain of God', 20 (1967) 129-148 or L. J. Kuyper, 'The suffering and repentance of God', 22 (1969) 257-277.

[2] W. McWilliams, 'Divine suffering in contemporary theology', *Scottish Journal of Theology* 33 (1980) 35.

impassibility in his essay 'The need for a Scriptural, therefore a neo-classical theism'.[3]

The main problem affecting this development has often been stated to be that of reconciling the immutability of God with the incarnation. Although this is quite understandable in the light of the vivid way the reality of the eternal Son of God assuming flesh propulses the notion of divine change to the forefront of theological debate, it is perhaps not *the* central theological issue involved. After all, immutability stood unquestioned until the 19th century, in spite of the incarnation. After Hegel, the former ontology of immutability was replaced by an idealist ontology of the becoming of being. The living God came to be identified as a mutable God, with christological extensions in kenoticism. Moltmann's view of change in God can be placed in this general drift, with antecedents in the thought of Dorner or Thomasius, and Barth or Brunner.

2.The Identity of the Reformed Tradition

The nature of the reformed tradition with regard to the immutability of God is not immediately clear. Is it the same as the classical Christian tradition? Is it a carbon copy of classical theism in the Thomist sense? Did reformed theologians fall foul of Greek metaphysics and succumb to abstract ways of talking about God? Such questions, valid in themselves, lie outside the scope of our enquiry. For convenience's sake we will suppose that, allowing for a few variants with classical theism, reformed theologians, at least in their great majority, hold a view of immutability which is largely synonymous with the classical view. We will take Moltmann's criticisms of classical theism as applying to the reformed tradition, which he also addresses directly on several occasions, particularly in *God in Creation* .

---

[3] C. Pinnock in *Perspectives in Evangelical Theology* ed. K. Kantzer and S. Gundry (Grand Rapids: Baker, 1979).

God and Change, Immanence and Transcendence
1. What is meant by the immutability of God?
A definition as useful as any is that of J.H. Heidegger, given in the context of reformed scholasticism:
> Immutability is that attribute of God by which He alone is *per se* and *a se*, in actuality and in potency, devoid of all succession, change or variation, remaining the same eternally without even the faintest shadow of transmutation.[4]

It could be complemented with that of Quenstedt:
> Immutability is the perpetual identity of the divine essence and all its perfections, with the absolute negation of motion, either physical or ethical.[5]

The root of this notion is the spirituality and simplicity of God which have their correlates in aseity and immutability. God's nature, attributes and purposes remain ever unchanged. God lives in timeless eternity. It is heartily denied that this implies immobility. As R.L. Dabney stated: 'God is not active but activity'. He adds, after affirming the perfect harmony of immutability with other divine attributes: 'scarcely any attribute is more clearly manifested to the reason than God's immutability'.[6]

---

[4] Quoted by H. Heppe, *Reformed Dogmatics* (Grand Rapids: Baker, 1978) 67.

[5] Quoted by R.A. Muller in his useful study 'Incarnation, immutability, and the case for classical theism', *Westminster Theological Journal* 45 (1983) 25.

[6] R. L. Dabney, *Systematic Theology* (Grand Rapids: Zondervan, 1972, 1878) 43, 45.

2. *An attempt to elucidate the question*

The fundamental problem raised concerning divine immutability is probably not that of creation or even incarnation. Would it not be rather naïve to think that theology had been so blinkered by hellenistic divine immobility as to be unaware of the tension generated by this concept in relation to other *loci* of theology? The real question seems to be rather : what view of the relation of the transcendence and immanence of God permits divine immutability and divine activity to be articulated without contradiction?

To state the problematic another way: without *some* form of immanence, a positive relation between God and the world could play no rôle in human knowledge and life. It would be impossible to speak of divine immanence or even of a transcendent being. If God were purely transcendent there could be no link between the world and God.

The question of change in God, or its correlate divine passibility, involves a certain conception of divine immanence because it is only in the context of divine contact with finite reality that change could be perceived with relation to God. However, if immanence implied mutability in any form, a modified view of divine transcendence would then follow. For instance, if God aged with time, or altered his decisions, one would be obliged to conclude that time existed in God or that God was influenceable. This would have profound implications for the theological concept of divine transcendence.

Moltmann and metaphysics

In considering Moltmann in the light of the reformed tradition, we shall retain this one point to elucidate his view of God and change: how does he conceive of the nature of divine transcendence and immanence and their relation? Our intention is not to reply to Moltmann, but to indicate at what points divergences arise in relation to classical theism.

In this section, two subjects can be reviewed: Moltmann's criticism of classical theism, as he believes that the marriage of ontology and theology needs revision, and his own presentation of the relation of God and world.

1. Criticism of the apathetic God

In his works on the Trinity and the creation Moltmann makes concerted attacks on what he calls 'Christian monotheism'. Although Christian theologians may affirm their trinitarian concerns, in fact they easily fall prey to an undifferentiated way of considering the divine being. Whether he presents traditional theism's God as supreme substance or more recent personalistic re-statements of God as absolute subject, his criticism is invariable. These views suppose a hierarchical (masculine) notion of God in which God is considered above the world, and creation is made an object. Such thinking no longer has real relevance for the mentality of the age in which we live.

Fundamental to this criticism is the idea that classical theism in its various species implies some kind of abstraction. God is defined in terms of absolutes which are out of joint with historical realities. Divine impassibility is formulated by taking created reality and eliding all that is mutable, relative, or subject to suffering or change.[7] Moltmann thinks that Chalcedonian christology verges on docetism,[8] because everything associated with suffering or change is attributed to the human nature of Christ and abstracted from his divinity:

---

[7] On impassibility, see the survey given by R. Bauckham, '"Only the suffering God can help": divine passibility in modern theology', *Themelios* 9 (1984:3) 6-12.

[8] *The Crucified God* (London : SCM, 1974) 227f; *The Trinity and the Kingdom of God* (London : SCM, 1981) 13-20, 139ff.

> If this concept of God is applied to Christ's death on the
> cross, the cross *must* be evacuated of deity, for by
> definition God cannot suffer and die. He is pure
> causality.... The God who was the subject of suffering
> could not be truly God.[9]

How can a self-sufficient God be involved in the dramas
of human existence? An immutable or impassible God
cannot have a part in the passion of Christ, nor be
reconcilied with the biblical view of the prophets who
speak poignantly of the divine pathos implied in the
involvement of God with a suffering people. Moreover, an
immutable God cannot be a God who loves freely. Dabney
affirms immutability to be most reasonable; Moltmann
would probably reply that this is the case because he is
taken up with the notion of a static God, which is
irreconcilable with the scandal of the divine abandonment
of the Son of God at the cross.

Moltmann is arguing rather forcefully that the
transcendent God cannot be other than the immanent God
revealed on Golgotha. Classical theism is trapped in
contradictions, as God's transcendence cannot be
reconciled with his immanence. These aspects of the
divine nature, rather than being contradictory, are to be
stated as complementary.

2. Divine reciprocation
Moltmann's proposition is that this sort of abstraction be
replaced by reciprocation. We must see the passion of God
in Christ and the passion of Christ in God.[10] The Bible
speaks not only of the experience man has of God, but also
of that which God has with man. God suffers with, by and
for us. This theme is repeated almost *ad nauseam* in *The
Trinity and the Kingdom of God*. The cross reveals the

---

[9] *The Crucified God*, 214f.
[10] *The Trinity and the Kingdom of God*, (London: SCM, 1981) 47ff.

essence of God. God offers himself to himself in eternal suffering love. Divinity is not separated from humanity, nor humanity from divinity.[11] Likewise, when the doctrine of the creation is formulated, we are not to set over the Creator against his objective work, but to conceive of the world as inhabited by God.[12] To quote:

> The relationship between God and the world has a reciprocal character, because this relationship must be seen as a living one.[13]

From this perspective, when the relation of God and the world is discussed, an apathetic God does not satisfy the demands of the human situation, but only a God who suffers passionately with the world, assuming transience and death. A God incapable of suffering is also a God incapable of love ; love opens the divinity to suffering.[14]

A further weakness in traditional theism is its monotheism which, although attractive for present inter-faith dialogue, cannot do justice to the trinitarian revelation alluded to in the New Testament texts. A reciprocal view of God permits the development of a trinitarian doctrine of God in which the *opera trinitatis ad extra* and the *opera trinitatis ad intra* are related. The external works of God, creation, incarnation and glorification are bound up, says Moltmann, with his internal works-:

> In fact it is not a question of the 'works' of the Trinity 'outwards' and 'inwardly' at all; it is a matter of the 'sufferings' which correspond reciprocally to the works.[15]

'Outwards' and 'inwards' constitutes a scholastic distinction: what we are talking about is the 'suffering *of*

---

[11] *Ibid.*, 50-53.

[12] *God in Creation*, 13.

[13] *The Trinity and the Kingdom of God*, 98, *cf.* 59, 105, 111, 119, 127, 161.

[14] *Ibid.*, 23.

[15] *Ibid.*, 98, *cf.* 93, 115.

God' in which the barrier erected by this distinction is broken down.

This point could bear a good deal of discussion, but what does it mean? Moltmann clarifies its implication:

> I find myself bound to surrender the traditional distinction between the immanent and the economic Trinity.[16]

Contrary to the Augustinian addage: the Godhead is inwardly three distinct persons outwardly united in action, Moltmann says that God is divided and differentiated outwardly. The cross has a retroactive effect on the Father which causes infinite pain.

However, the end of the line has not yet been reached, as Moltmann carries his notion of reciprocity further. Rather than speaking of the acts of God affecting his being, the inner divine passion should be considered as primary in determining his action. Divine passion does not impinge upon the Son alone, from the limited perspective of his humanity, but is theopathically trinitarian. God does not suffer from lack of being but from superabundance of being. The passionate suffering of intra-divine love spills over into his external acts.[17]

In this perspective, Moltmann speaks not only of trinitarian *perichoresis,* but also of the reciprocal inhabitation of God and the world. All relations that are analogical to God reflect trinitarian *perichoresis* as God is in the world and the world is in God. Thus Moltmann links the divine trinitarian community with the human horizontal one in common progression toward reconciliation. The soteriology of Moltmann joins divine and human life in a process moving from suffering to glorification which mirrors

---

16 *Ibid.,* 160.
17 *Ibid.,* 40.

intra-divine relations. Moltmann calls this a 'social doctrine of the Trinity.'[18]

However, one point of clarification is needed. If 'God has a history' because of *perichoresis* , and the divinity can even be said to experience pain,[19] Moltmann makes a distinction between the suffering of the Father and that of the Son. 'The Son suffers dying (erleidet das Sterben), the Father suffers the death (erleidet den Tod) of the Son.' So the Father suffers the death of his fatherhood and the Son becomes fatherless.[20] By distinguishing the different sufferings of God rather than the divinity and humanity of the person and work of the Son, Moltmann attempts to hold together the active participation of God in human history and some form of independence from the threat of total passibility and mutability. Death is experienced *in* God, but it is not the death *of* God. However, whether this distinction is more than linguistic is highly debatable.

The History of the Passionate God
Although Moltmann's thought may have evolved substantially since the *Theology of Hope* (1964), its fundamental perspective has been maintained. Reality is seen as dynamic and historical, and temporality, provisionality and change are fundamental. The order of the divine decrees relative to creation, incarnation and eschatology undergoes reorganisation.

The end of history with transfiguration and cosmic reconciliation is really its proper beginning:
>   Justification... is not a restoration of man springing from his beginning ; it is the new beginning of his becoming man at his end... part of a universal transfiguration of

---

18 *Ibid.*, 34.
19 *The Future of Creation* (Philadelphia: Fortress, 1979) 93.
20 *The Crucified God*, 243. See the article by A. König, 'Le Dieu crucifié?' in *Hokhma* 17 (1981).

the passing world... to be understood as its beginning.[21]

This dynamic is given substance in *God in Creation* :

God decides for the kingdom first of all, and then for creation. Consequently it is the kingdom that determines creation and creation is the real promise of the kingdom.[22]

More description could be given at this point and many comments made, but we shall restrict the discussion to three areas: the historical process itself, the nature of creation and the notion of the divine decree.

1. *The historical process*

The orientation of reality procedes toward the pole of God's eschatological self-deliverance, when he will be all in all, from his self-subjection to suffering. This movement takes place in God. It has its trinitarian roots in the self-moderation of God, understood as divine humility before the creation. Likewise, in the original creative act, God limits himself and creates the world from nothing. In the incarnation and the abandonment of the cross Christ enters the original nothingness of creation, the space for finitude in himself, in order to fill it with his presence. Through the resurrection, finitude is brought into the light of new creation.[23] Between the two poles lies the history of God with man which holds the promise of future transfiguration.

2. *Creation as self-limitation*

Creation is not strictly outside of God, but takes place within the divinity. By his self-withdrawal God makes space in his being for finitude and history. As God limits himself he is distinct from the world's contingency. Yet, at the same time, he creates a world that 'corresponds to

---

21 *The Future of Creation*, 170.

22 *God in Creation*, 81; *cf.* 277.

23 *The Future of Creation*, 117-120; *God in Creation*, 213.

him'. In this way Moltmann seeks to solve the old problem of how, if God is self-sufficient, there can be an *ad extra*. However, Moltmann's formulations may be as obscure as anything engendered by classic theism, as when he says-:

> God withdraws himself in order to go out of himself. Eternity breathes itself in so as to breathe out the Spirit of life.[24]

3. The divine decree
Moltmann replaces the free decision of barthian supra-lapsarianism with an eschatologically-determined supra-creationism. Creation is not necessary because of a divine decree, which would imply a verbal distinction between God's being and his decretive act, and posits a 'before and after' in God. God is creator by divine life. The divine love of Father, Son and Spirit is expressed when God's trinitarian perfections overflow and create a movement culminating in the cosmic sabbath. In freedom and in love God decides for the kingdom, incarnation and creation. The same love produces different effects within the divinity and in the divine creation.

Immanence and Transcendence in Moltmann
Each of these aspects illustrates briefly how divine immanence and transcendence are redefined by Moltmann. The notion of divine self-limitation implies *some* form of mutability in God, although its implications are not entirely clear-:

> Time is an interval in eternity, finitude is a space in infinity, and freedom is a concession of the eternal love.[25]

In fact, it is no longer exact to speak about divine transcendence and immanence as such, for this supposes a distinction between God and the world which sets them over against each other. In a section on 'the immanence of

---

24 *The Trinity and the Kingdom of God*, 111; *God in Creation*, 87.
25 *Ibid.*

God in the world' at the start of *God in Creation*,
Moltmann affirms that the immanent and the transcendent
God are one and the same. Creation is a tension which
exists immanently in God, a community of life between
God and his creatures in which unilateral, multilateral and
reciprocal relations exist. But God is not only 'outside of
himself' as he makes himself immanent to the world, he is
also 'in himself' in his self-identification as he transcends
the world. Immanence and transcendence are synonymous
with the concepts of divine participation and anticipation.
Creation exists in God and is open to God in its future
orientation.[26]

Evaluation from a Reformed Perspective

Two fundamental commentaries, which may seem rather
surprising by their radicality, can be made in order to
crystallise the contrast between Moltmann's view of
divine change and that of classical theism.[27]

*1. Moltmann's view of divine immanence stands in a
contradictory relation to what is affirmed about divine
transcendence in classical theism*

By this we mean that what Moltmann affirms about the
nature of divine immanence so contradicts the concept of
transcendence of classical theism that the two affirmations
cannot be harmonised. To adopt Moltmann's views of
divine immanence inevitably involves abandoning reformed
theology's view of divine transcendence. This proposition
could be verified in several areas, but three illustrations
have been selected.

Firstly, reformed theology locates the origin of *creation*
in a transcendent divine decision. This implies what
Cornelius Van Til called the 'full-bucket problem': God is

---

26 *God in Creation*, 266.
27 J. Frame, *The Doctrine of the Knowledge of God* (Phillipsburg
NJ: Presbyterian and Reformed, 1987) 13-18.

self-sufficient and yet decides to create a world distinct from himself.[28] For Moltmann, creation is immanent in God and God is immanent in creation. This implies that all change exists in God and that God is present in all change. Reformed theology would reply that because of divine transcendence, all change implies divine activity, but divine activity need not imply change in God. In making creation an extension in God of a divine self-distinction, Moltmann has not answered the question of how self-distinction can exist without self-determination. Moreover, a criticism commonly formulated against Moltmann is that he does not seem to have elucidated how divine transcendence is different from the self-transcendence of the world-process.[29]

Secondly, for reformed theology *suffering and sin* are intrusions in God's good creation. They exist as ethical and existential consequences of human disobedience. Moltmann criticises this position as a superficial anthropological approach. Future salvation is not simply a return to a primal condition. There seems to be little place in Moltmann's thought for a historical fall and a passage from grace to wrath in divine-human relations because of sin. Consequently he links suffering to ontological finitude as a pre-condition for the opening of creation to the future of God. Suffering in the world corresponds to the pathos of God, who limits himself in order to orientate reality toward the fulness of all things. However, if this sort of reciprocity between immanence and transcendence is established with regard to suffering, how can it be avoided for sin and evil? Moltmann's view of immanence seems to lead him

---

[28] C. Van Til, *An Introduction to Systematic Theology* (Philadelphia: Westminster Seminary, 1971) ch.3.
[29] B.J.Walsh gives an excellent critique of Moltmann in his article 'Theology of hope and the doctrine of creation: an appraisal of Jürgen Moltmann', *Evangelical Quarterly* 59 (1987:1) 53-76.

logically to diametrically oppose the reformed doctrine of
the transcendent righteousness of God.

Finally, if passion precedes action in God and history
takes place in God, redemption no longer has the sense of
divine re-storation. Remission, redemption, renewal,
regeneration, re-creation, all lose the force of the prefix
're-', which is a characteristic feature of reformed
soteriology.[30] If, as the structure of Moltmann's thought
would seem to indicate, the ultimate transfiguration of
reality is the foundation of the incarnation, which is in turn
the foundation of creation, then does not the immanence of
God become necessary to divine being and the Son's death
become essential to the inner dynamic of the Trinity? This
is the opposite of Federal theology's *pactum salutis*, which
is a transcendent act of divine liberty. For reformed
theology, God is immanent because of his transcendence,
not the contrary. For Moltmann, because divine
immanence implies change in God, it also implies change
in trinitarian rôles. The model Father, Son and Spirit is no
longer the unique model of the ontological Trinity. God
himself is in situation and in mutation.[31] Furthermore, in
classical reformed theology transcendence and immanence
are categories which apply to the relation of God and the
world and are therefore creationally determined. In
Moltmann they lose their creational reference and become
metaphysical categories. In spite of all the anti-
metaphysical rhetoric, in this respect his thought-structure
appears to be more metaphysical than that of classical
theism!

2. *Moltmann's view of divine transcendence stands in a
contradictory relation to what is affirmed about divine
immanence in classical theism*

---

[30] *Ibid.*, 61.
[31] *The Trinity and the Kingdom of God*, 202ff.

By this we mean, as above, that Moltmann's affirmations about the nature of divine transcendence contradict the immanence concept of classical theism. To adopt Moltmann's views of divine transcendence inevitably involves abandoning a reformed idea of divine immanence.

The sort of transcendence Moltmann refers to is, by all accounts, different from the incommunicable transcendence of the reformed tradition. This means it contradicts the reformed view of immanence.

First of all, Moltmann's notion of reciprocity appears to undermine the traditional *distinction between Creator and creature*. By talking in terms of community Moltmann metamorphoses the alterity of divine transcendence in such a way as to make God depend for his experience on finite reality. Thus *perichoresis* within the Trinity is taken as the hermeneutic principle not only for what happens in God but also for what happens between God and the world and in the world. This point of view seems to forget that divine *perichoresis* implies *homoousia*, which is the condition for the Son's action in creation without the implication that creation exists in God. For Moltmann's theory to hold good, he would have to establish *homoousia* between God and the world, but he cannot do this and avoid pantheism. This point alone shows how far Moltmann's view of transcendence is opposed to the immanence of reformed theism in which God is revealed in creation without being analogous to it.

Furthermore, Moltmann's view of transcendence seems to make *God totally knowable*, at least in some respects. One of the most infuriating things about his idealistic constructions regarding the divinity is their lack of

theological humility.[32] Just as a computer knows every
chess move one makes, Moltmann seems to know in
advance just where God is going and in a way very
different from that of biblical eschatology. 'The nucleus of
everything that Christian theology says about 'God' is to
be found in the Christ event'.[33] But how do we know this,
or any other of the things he affirms about transcendent
reality? Has not Moltmann made a unjustifiable leap when
he affirms that when the *Son* experiences and suffers from
sin, *God* experiences something which belongs essentially
to the world?[34] Such assurance in charting the depths of
God's inner life is unjustifiable in the light of the mysteries
of Scripture. He seems to talk about God like one might
talk about other human beings. This is contrary to the view
of traditional theism expressed in the reformed tradition
which affirms that God is anonymous[35], but has many
immanent names, none of which correspond to divine
reality in univocal fashion. In his revelation God
appropriates human attributes. His immanence reveals
him to be the incomprehensible One.

Finally, as far as *trinitarian relations* are concerned,
Moltmann seeks to explain immanent worldly events in
terms of inner-divine acts. Thus the whole course of
history is re-interpreted and the biblical history is turned
on end. Events correspond to the divine being and its
passions. This stands in contrast with the traditional view
of creation-fall-redemption in which, to use Bavinck's
expression, the divine decree effects nothing in itself.[36]
God's immanence does not restrict the contingency of the

32 Along these lines see the comments of J.B.Webster, 'Jürgen
Moltmann: Trinity and Suffering', *Evangel,* Summer 1985, 6 and J.
McIntyre in *Scottish Journal of Theology* 41 (1988) 270-273.
33 *The Crucified God,* 205.
34 *The Future of Creation,* 93.
35 H. Bavinck, *The Doctrine of God* (Grand Rapids: Baker, 1951) 90.
36 *Ibid.,* 399, 378, 370; Walsh, *art. cit.* 60ff.

world which includes human actions and events. What is difficult to explain on Moltmann's terms is: why did God create rather than immediately transfiguring the world, why was the incarnate Adam made and not the incarnate Christ? In what way do sin and pain correspond to God?

Conclusion
What is missed in Moltmann's re-structuration of theism, subtle and complex, intriguing and masterly though it may be, is the paradox of the *and,* the mystery of reformed theism's transcendence and immanence.

For Moltmann this *is* that; all is in God and God in all. God is rationally explained and yet remains totally irrational. Ultimately *nothing changes* in respect to God, because the end appears to be the starting-point of the divine life. However, if time is a part of eternity will not this *processus* be commenced ever anew? And therefore will not *everything change* eternally in God?

Are we not caught on the horns of an irreconcilable dilemma in which necessity and contingency are equally ultimate in God? Can *this* divinity be the transcendent Lord and the victorious Saviour of the Scriptures?

WEAK CHURCH, WEAK GOD

THE CHARGE OF ANTHROPOMORPHISM

DAVID COOK

The problems of religious language were attacked directly by Aquinas with his doctrine of analogy. There are two basic forms of analogy. There is the analogy of proportionality. This form suggests that one may use analogies of proportion to describe the attributes of God as in the same way proportional to his nature as the qualities of human beings and other creatures are proportional to their natures. The other form of analogy is that of attribution. For this approach to work one requires a primary term in the analogy. If one is drawing an analogy between God and man then there must be some priority. If we are talking of wisdom, then man's wisdom is a reflection of God's wisdom. God's wisdom is thus the primary term in the analogy. Both forms of analogy are not without problem. The analogy of proportionality faces the difficulty not so much in the analogy itself as in being able to start the analogy. How does one know of the attribute in the first place? This objection may have a response to it: that is, to suggest that all language is an expression of prior experience and thus analogy is no worse than other language forms. The empiricist retort must be that for ordinary experience language problems can be overcome by going back to experience. The empiricist is sceptical as to whether God can be experienced at all, far less talked about. A further problem with analogies of proportion is the necessity to specify exactly the relationship of the two things claimed to be proportional. Obviously human attributes are not exactly equivalent to divine attributes. The question is, how different is different? In what way are they like divine attributes? Do we not need to know this before any analogy of proportion will work?

For the analogy of attribution to work, again one needs some prior direct knowledge of God's wisdom which is not by analogy. If one tries to use some other primary term, like creation, then it is difficult to see how it helps us arrive at God. It starts from within the created order and stretches to a point beyond or above that order. It is clear that the problems of analogy of an appropriate way of talking about God reduce in the end to problems about how we know and experience God and thus are able to talk about God and our experience. Where the analogy method is in danger of breaking down is in the claim that there is a sense in which God is like anything human at all. All descriptions of God are seen as attempts to stretch human concepts on the basis of likeness to the level of the transcendent and divine. The question remains whether such an exercise is possible given the differences between God and all things human.

The use of analogy was one kind of solution to the problem of anthropomorphism. We shall ask whether the ideas of the weakness of God and of the suffering of God are not guilty of the charge of anthropomorphism.

The Charge of Reductionism

The abortion debate is bedevilled by endless discussions about when life truly begins. It is as if the debaters imagine that to establish the magic moment of life's origin will in itself also impart the value which is to be attached to human life at its very different stages and in its very different contexts. The search for the magic moment looks to the moments of fertilization, implantation, quickening, viability, birth, full term or independent existence as possible bases for the application of an ethic which does justice to the sanctity of human life. There are serious problems with the selection of each and every such magic moment to such an extent that many wonder whether there is not a basic reductionism involved in the very search itself. Human life ought not to be segmented and partitioned. It must be seen in its continuum and in its totality. There is no one moment which has significance over and against every other moment. Human life is continuous and ought to be valued in relation to that whole and continuum rather than in terms of parts.

We shall examine whether the ideas of the weakness and suffering of God are guilty of a form of reductionism.

The Charge of Conformity
J.B. Phillips' translation of Paul's injunction in Romans 12: 2 is 'Don't let the world squeeze you into its mould'. One of the constant complaints against theology is that it has done just that. It has allowed in particular the philosophies and ideologies of the day to shape and mould the expression of theology in such as way as to do harm to theological truth. For as the flaws in the philosophies and ideologies became evident then it seemed that not only the theological expression must be rejected, but the theological content itself. The classic example is that of the influence of Aristotle on Aquinas and the problems raised by making theological truth appear to depend on Aristotelian physics.

This critique of conformity is one key weapon in the armoury of those who seek to embrace the ideas of the weakness and suffering of God, but it may be that they themselves have fallen into the same trap. We shall explore whether or not they are guilty of the charge of conformity to the ideologies and philosophies of the day.

The Charge of Omission
Robert Schuller of 'The Crystal Cathedral' fame was once challenged by a Scripture Union worker from Singapore as to the absence of any talk of sin in his preaching and ministry. His response was instructive: 'I don't believe in dwelling on negativities.'

It is always easy to accuse any theological expression of the charge of omission and failure to include some ideas, references, or themes. But the charge against those who embrace the ideas of the weakness and suffering of God is that they have omitted any adequate treatment of the nature and seriousness of sin.

The Charge of Presuppositions and the Need for Change

It is instructive to ask of a writer against whom or what he is reacting. It is equally instructive to enquire as to the presuppositions being held by a writer. Each of us has a point from and by which to lever the world. All of us take certain things for granted and make some basic assumptions. Debate often focuses thus on the adequacy of any presuppositions and what such presuppositions ought to be.

Those who propound the ideas of the weakness and suffering of God are challenging certain traditionally accepted theological presuppositions. The adequacy of these presuppositions is quite properly open to debate and discussion. But any demand for the jettisoning of these traditional presuppositions and for their replacement by a new set requires two things: first that the case for a change is overwhelmingly obvious; second, that the new set will be far superior to the former presuppositions and not merely resolve the problems raised, but avoid major new problems of their own.

We shall examine whether the need for presuppositional change has been made evident and whether the new proposal is more adequate. In particular, some of the presuppositions about theodicy will be explored.

We shall not deal directly with the impassibility of God nor attempt to do justice to any full blown doctrine of the church which would be necessary to balance the title given for the lecture. Rather we focus on the kind of analysis offered by Jurgen Moltmann and the themes of weakness and suffering imputed by him and others to God and on our knowledge of God.

Anthropomorphism
Titles like *The Human Face of God* and *The Crucified God* are indicative of the notion of the weakness of God. In a later section we shall examine something of the background to this idea, but at the moment it is the question of what sense we are to attach to it which is the focus.

When the cancer patient is weak and helpless, he or she often asks the Director of the Hospice in Oxford, Why me? His reply is rather brutal. 'Why not? Why should you be immune? This is just the way the world is.' Weakness here is simply the result of the circumstances we find ourselves in. We have no control over these situations or circumstances. We are victims, often through no particular fault of our own. There may also be situations where we are now weak as a result of actions which have led directly to this weakness, as with some AIDS sufferers. These results may have been technically foreseeable, yet the awfulness of the weakness is partly in that we could not easily avoid the inevitable results of the way the world is and functions.

This weakness is part of what it means to be human and to live in a world limited by time and space. In theodical terms it comes very near to the idea of metaphysical evil, though actual suffering and felt weakness are a necessary corollary.

There is a more direct sense of weakness which is the result of our own action and sin. If I smoke forty cigarettes and drink three bottles of whisky a day, it will be no surprise if I end up a weakened wreck of a human being.

73

The results here are not merely the outcome of the way the world happens to be, but the direct result of the way the world was designed to be. In other words we live in a moral universe, where God has so ordered the nature of things and of people that what we sow we reap. There are inevitable moral consequences for our action and failures to act and these may well have a direct physically painful form. My sin leads directly to my weakness.

There is a sense in which weakness may imply being easily affected or even too easily affected. Moltmann is careful to eschew this kind of weakness in relation to Jesus. In talking of Christ's experience in the Garden of Gethsemane he says, 'But it would also be foolish to view him as a sensitive weakling who was overcome by lachrymose self-pity in the face of bodily torment and his swiftly approaching death' (*The Power of the Powerless* p.1170) yet there is still a sense of weakness, which in classical literature is described as 'womanly', which I presume would now be called sexist.

This leads to a notion of weakness which is really a sense of vulnerability. It is the capacity to be affected and an openness which is usually described as sensitivity. The weak person here is not unaffected by people but feels with them and is readily and easily affected by them.

There is also the sense of weakness which implies ineffectiveness and inability to cope. It is the sort of weakness that means when the going gets tough we know that we cannot rely on that person. He or she is likely to go to pieces at any moment and will have to be 'carried' through the situation.

It is obvious that there are many different nuances bound up in the idea of weakness which may well have parallels in the idea of suffering when applied to God. The question is which descriptions are being proferred and which rejected, and, more importantly, by what criteria.

In the case of Christ, it is clear that both the actual physical weakness which comes through hunger, thirst, pain and suffering as well as the entering in to the conditions of space, time and human being are part of Jesus' condescension. Our Christmas carols delight in accounts of the helplessness of the child in the manger. Likewise the newer song from Graham Kendrick points to the helpless babe who came as the servant king.

But when we try to apply the description of 'weakness' to God, can we make sense of the Father becoming subject to the conditions which he set and yet retaining, not merely his eternal fatherhood, but any meaningful distinction and differentiation from Jesus, the Son? More fundamentally, can we talk of 'weakness' in relation to God in the same way as we talk of 'weakness' in relation to ourselves and the church? The crunch here is in determining which ideas come first. Do we begin with some understanding and experience of the weakness which is part and parcel of our human situation, especially when we suffer, and then apply these attributes and experiences to God? Are we here in danger of an anthropomorphism which makes God in our image? If there is any justice in the criticism, it would seem that such an account of God may well give too much power and significance to circumstances, to sin and to the power of the Evil One. The danger is of a slide to a setting where the sin is more important than the cure for sin, the evil more important than the solution to evil, and the weakness more important than the transformation of that weakness, where strength is made perfect in weakness.

In the end the fear is that talk of our suffering and weakness in the same breath and terms as the suffering and weakness of Christ, never mind of God, can seem to imply that all such suffering and weakness is of the same order and significance.

When we are called to take up the cross daily, to imitate Christ and to suffer, we must not imagine that our suffering is of the same order as that of Christ, nor that our suffering is somehow redemptive. If Christ's sacrifice on the cross was genuinely once for all there can be no sense in which we can add to, or indeed take away from, that finished and completed work. The call to be like is not the call to be. The weakness of our humanity and the suffering we endure is not redemptive or salvific. A theology of works lurks just around those corners.

But there is another form in which the desire to describe God in terms of our human characteristics, qualities and situations is expressed. Moltmann in *The Crucified God* (pp. 219–227) argues that the theology of the crucified God gives a way forward in relation to the problems of suffering which avoids the unsatisfactoriness of 'metaphysical atheism' and 'protest atheism'. For Moltmann the crucified God shares in the suffering of the world and in the suffering of Jesus takes up humanity's protest against suffering in the world. Thus God for us becomes the human God who cries with us and intercedes for us with his cross in situations where human beings are dumb. It is not quite clear at whom the cry is aimed, or whether there is supposedly some virtue in crying or even the cry itself, but this all sounds suspiciously as if this is the God we need. Later we shall see some account of the motives behind the ideas of the weakness of God, but that of satisfying our need in the midst of our suffering seems clearly involved. This is simply anthropomorphism and has no warrant in itself. It must still be judged by whether or not it does justice to the nature of God in himself and not merely the creation of God in our image to satisfy, if indeed it will, our needs and desires.

Moltmann can take this kind of step and make it seem that to suffer is in itself a great virtue. Nowadays people like to overlook the suffering that is part of every great passion. People want to be perfectly happy, so they suppress suffering. They stifle pain, and rob themselves of feeling at the same time. Life without passion is poverty-stricken. Life without the readiness for suffering is shallow. We have to overcome both our fear of passion and our fear of suffering. Otherwise hope cannot be born again (*The Power of the Powerless*, p.115). If taken literally and applied to God, we are doing him a favour in allowing that he suffers and gains the helpful insights which apparently cannot be learned any other way than the hard one. Such an account of suffering comes very near to a kind of glorying in suffering itself and makes suffering and weakness almost ends in themselves.

A further danger of anthropomorphism arises in the understanding of personal love implicit in talking of the weakness and suffering of God. It is argued that if God is personal love then he must be open to suffering which is a necessary part of loving relationships. The point at issue here is the basis of our understanding of personal love. Do we begin from the human perspective and then try to stretch our concept by applying it to the divine? Alternatively, do we take our starting point as the love of God in his own unique personhood, which love is only understood as it is revealed according to his eternal nature and the ground of itself. Paul Helm has offered a critique of arguments levelled against the idea of a timeless person. He argues that 'it is consistent to ascribe to a timeless God powers which we normally say that only persons have even though such powers are not what all persons have' (*Eternal God*, p.72). I think it is possible to mount a defence of the idea of love in an eternal being along the helpful lines Helm uses in relation to purpose.

It does not follow for the claim that an eternal being does not purposefully initiate actions that such a being does not have purposes. He may have timeless purposes, purposes which are brought about in time, that is, in the temporal order of his creation. These effects, it may be supposed, come about as a result of the eternal being's purposes, but they do not come about after those eternal purposes, nor are they contemporaneous with them. The distinction between the eternal purposes and their effects is not a temporal distinction in the sense that certain actions occur after the formulation of the intention or purpose, but the distinction is a logical one. The purpose is not identical with the effect, and the effect comes about as a result of the purpose. The effect may be a physical change, but the purpose is not physical and is timeless (*Eternal God*, p.62.)

There is here the possible basis for a parallel argument about eternal personal love which avoids the anthropomorphism, which seems an inevitable part of talk of the crucified God.

The first charge against the ideas of the weakness and suffering of God is that of anthropomorphism.

Parts and Wholes – Reductionism
The second charge is that of so emphasizing one aspect of truth that truth itself may become distorted.

How do we know the nature of God? There are at least two different aspects to this question. The first is, What is the nature of God? and the second is, How do we know God and his nature? These are quite different issues from the question how we might seek to do justice to God and his nature by finding adequate vehicles to express who what he is.

At one level, the history of theology seems like a constant set of corrections where one aspect of God's nature has been expressed to the exclusion of other aspects. Indeed, that is something of the motivating force behind talk of the weakness and suffering of God. But we need to consider how we know that nature in its total context. Christian theology believes in revelation. God reveals himself to human kind. The problem is whether there is a unique revelation of God's nature in the cross and what that revelation is. If there is such a unique revelation in the cross, how does that cohere with what else God has revealed of himself and his nature?

John Stott in his masterly account of the cross of Christ suggests that God does reveal his nature in the cross. He reveals his glory – for suffering is the path to glory. He reveals his justice – for Christ's sacrifice of atonement demonstrates God's justice. He reveals his love – for God proves his love in history through the death of his son (*The Cross of Christ*, chapter 8). It is this kind of analysis which Moltmann takes further, following Luther, and which enables him to say that Luther's theology of the cross 'is not a single chapter in theology, but the key signature for all Christian theology' (*The Crucified God*, p. 72).

McCleod Campbell produced an important corrective to one-sided emphases in his famous or infamous *The Nature of the Atonement*. The necessity of the incarnation itself as part of a proper understanding of the revelation of God in Christ, while important, did not go far enough. The desire to fasten onto one moment in the history of Christ always runs the danger of failing to do justice to all of his life and nature. Christ needs to be understood in creation, incarnation, redemption, resurrection, in his high priestly ministry, in judgement and in glory. So too with the nature of God. God reveals himself and his nature in creation – in the act, form and content of that creation. Who and what God is is shown in creation. Likewise in Providence and history. God reveals himself in his activity in the world and in history, especially in his dealings with his own people, the Jews. God reveals himself through the law and the prophets, both of which point to the nature of God and express that nature to humanity. God reveals himself fully in Jesus Christ. But it is surely in the totality of Jesus that God is revealed. It is in the birth, life, death, resurrection and glorification of Jesus that we are shown what God's nature is like. To stop at the cross would be only to tell part of the tale. At times hints that God reveals himself only properly in the cross is to undercut the history and record of God's revelation to and dealings with his people. It is also to reduce the significance of who and what Jesus is and his total ministry from creation to glory.

Moltmann, following Heschel and Kitamori recognizes that the Old Testament often describes the pain and suffering of God. As Richard Bauckham puts it, 'God is disappointed and distressed by his people's faithlessness: he is pained and offended by their lack of response to his love; he grieves over his people even when he must be angry with them (Jer. 31:30; Hos. 11:8–9); and because of his concern for them he himself suffers with them in their suffering (Is. 63:9)' (*Themelios* p.9, April 1986). Moltmann makes a similar point. 'If God has opened his heart in the covenant with his people, he is injured by disobedience and suffers in the people' (*The Crucified God*, p. 272). It is especially interesting here that Moltmann goes on to a discussion of the wrath of God where he takes particular pains to avoid anthropomorphism and distinguish between 'lower human emotions' and the 'category of the divine pathos' (*ibid.*, p.272).

Yet Moltmann in his critical account of protest atheism offers this analysis: 'a God who cannot suffer is poorer than any man. For a God who is incapable of suffering is a being who cannot be involved. Suffering and injustice do not affect him. And because he is so completely insensitive, he cannot be affected or shaken by anything. He cannot weep, for he has no tears. But the one who cannot suffer cannot love either. So he is a loveless being. Aristotle's God cannot love; he can only be loved by all non-divine beings by virtue of his perfection and beauty, and in this way draw them to him. The "unmoved Mover" is a "loveless Beloved"' (*The Crucified God*, p.222).

Later in the same chapter, Moltmann describes what happened on the cross of Christ. 'God is unconditional love, because he takes on himself grief at the contradiction in men and does not angrily suppress this contradiction. God allows himself to be forced out. God suffers, God allows himself to be crucified and is crucified, and in this consummates his unconditional love that is so full of hope' (*ibid.*, p.284).

There seems a tension here between the eternal nature of God as love and the idea of 'consummation' of his love, as if God's love is somehow incomplete until and unless he suffers on the cross. But that inevitably implies some previous inadequacy in God's love and that the experience of death on the cross in and of itself is sufficient to transform the unconsummated into the consummate.

Moltmann, however, claims that his account of the crucified God alone does justice to the doctrine of the Trinity and that only the doctrine of the Trinity makes sense of the weakness, suffering and crucifixion of God. Despite claims to test his argument that the 'Theology of the cross must be the doctrine of the Trinity and the doctrine of the Trinity must be the Theology of the cross, because otherwise the human, crucified God cannot be fully perceived' (*ibid.*, p.241).

One must ask whether Moltmann really does express the argument in any degree of sufficiency to enable us to see exactly what is meant and what grounds there are for such bold claims. The fear is that justice will neither be done to the Trinity nor to each Person in the Trinity and we will be offered a reductionistic account. Throughout, the risk in talk of the crucified God is of a fatal confusion between the crucified Son and the 'crucified Father', despite Moltmann's concern to distinguish the forms of suffering undergone by the Father and the Son. Moltmann argues that new converging trends in theological thought are concentrating on 'the question and the knowledge of God in the death of Christ on the cross and attempt to understand God's being from the death of Jesus' (p. 201). Again,

> As we may not assume that this death "does not affect" God, this death itself expresses God' (following Rahner). 'The death of Jesus is a statement of God about himself'. But to what degree is God himself 'concerned in' or 'affected by' the fate of Jesus on the cross (p. 202)?

And

> when the crucified Jesus is called the 'image of the invisible God' the meaning is that this is God, and God is like this. God is not greater than he is in this humiliation. God is not more glorious than he is in this self-surrender. God is not more powerful than he is in this helplessness. God is not more divine than he is in this humanity. The nucleus of everything that Christian Theology says about God is to be found in this Christ event. The Christ event on the cross is a God event. And conversely, the God event takes place on the cross of the risen Christ. Here God has not just acted externally, in his unattainable glory and eternity; here God has acted in himself and has gone on to suffer in himself. Here he himself is love with all his being (*The Crucified God*, p. 205).

Such speculation is, of course, interesting, but it is far from clear how we are to know what counts as evidence to establish or confute such claims and provide secure conclusions. How can we know what was going on in the heart and mind of God, as the Son cried out in the God forsakenness of the cross, 'My God, My God, why hast thou forsaken me?'

If indeed God did suffer on the cross, then God is the author of evil, as the one who requires satisfaction and propitiation, as well as the sufferer. It has been hard enough to distinguish the Father and the Son's role in the cross, without now adding some convoluted idea of self-negation, self-flagellation and self-inflicted injury.

The fear is of a failure to do justice to the different persons of the Trinity and instead to be guilty of reductionism. Yet elsewhere in *The Power of the Powerless* Moltmann is much more careful. In discussing Luther's heading of 'The struggle in Gethsemane' Moltmann states that the struggle is '... Christ's struggle with God. This was real agony. He overcame it through his self-surrender. That was His victory, and our hope' (p. 117). He then goes on to quote the writer to the Hebrews who said 'Far from God – even without God – he tasted death for us all' (2:9). And it is only here on the cross that Christ no longer addresses God intimately as 'Father', but calls him 'God'; quite officially, as if he were forced to doubt whether he really was the Son of God the Father.

What Christ was afraid of, what he wrestled with in Gethsemane, what he implored the Father to save him from, was not spared him. It happened on the cross. The Father forsook the Son and 'God is silent'. The Son was forsaken by the Father, rejected and cursed (p. 118).

Such careful distinguishing is in danger of collapse when Moltmann looks to Philippians 2 for our understanding of power. 'Normally we look upwards, to someone above us, when we are impressed by the glory. But in the case of

Jesus we have to look downwards. We discover his glory in his humbleness, his greatness in his poverty, his power in his self-surrender from the wretched manger in Bethlehem to the desolate cross on Golgotha' (*The Power of the Powerless*, p.24). Yet surely this is an inadequate reflection on the Philippian hymn. The movement is from the presence and equality of God and his glory to servanthood and death on a cross. But it is also a journey and movement instigated and empowered by God to the place of honour and Lordship, and all that for and to the glory of God.

The suspicion must be that talk of the weakness and suffering of God on the cross reduces both the view of the persons of the Trinity and of their own unique specific work and part in the totality of the divine plan and its execution.

The second charge is that of the danger of reductionism in relation to the nature of God and of the Trinity.

Conformity – Squeezed into the Mould?
Stott in a tantalizing section on the pain of God describes the way the Greek term and concept *apatheia* and the Latin adjective *impassibilia* were applied by philosophers to God. He then describes the uncritical acceptance of this by the early Greek Fathers of the church and their good, though apparently misguided, motives (*The Cross of Christ*, p. 330). Moltmann gives a more detailed account of the dependency, its inadequacy at the necessity for change (see pp. 227 and 267). Moltmann asserts that 'the adoption of the Greek philosophical concept of the "God incapable of suffering" by the early church led to difficulties in christology which only more recent theology has set out to overcome' (*The Crucified God*, p. 267). Bauckham takes the ground and motive for change a stage further in complexity by isolating the main factors in the move towards the modern doctrine of possibility as the context and scale of human suffering in the twentieth century, the

nature of God expressed in and through the prophets, an understanding of personal love in relation to God, the idea of the crucified God, and the relation between theodicy and divine suffering (see *Themelios*, April 1984 pp. 9-12).

One key aspect of the development of the idea of the weakness of God has been disquiet with the too ready acceptance of philosophical categories whose origin was not Judaeo-Christian and whose impact has been to make our understanding of God conform to alien, non-Christian patterns. God is not like that, it is claimed. This critique sounds exactly like that mounted by T.F. Torrance on liberal theology – that it has swallowed of out-moded subjectivist patterns of epistemology and ontology. Torrance offers a cure with a re-expression of objectivity founded on the same methods and approaches as modern science, especially physics. Even if Torrance makes his case for the necessity for change, he simply substitutes one form of scientific dependency for another. If modern science itself should one day be recognised as out-moded and inadequate, any theology whose expression and articulation were too closely and inextricably bound with that particular scientific perspective would be open to devastating criticism.

In the same kind of way the danger of this move to avoid conformity to and dependency on out-moded philosophical notions, is that it may simply substitute another set of largely unexamined and, in the long run, as well as perhaps in the short term, inadequate set of ideas. So much of the wider writing, especially from the pens of 'liberation theologians' reads like a plea for embracing a very particular set of political ideologies, which are highly debatable in themselves, and even more so in relation to God's nature. At other times, the writings of process theologians offer another philosophical basis for this new talk of God, but the philosophy of process is again far from self-evidently true. The pressure to speak in a meaningful

85

way to the modern situations of suffering seems again to set these situations as the ground of our understanding of God, rather than any attempt to do justice to God in and of himself.

In all these cases, God is put in particular boxes and his nature must be compatible with the contours of the boxes. But why? Are the boxes themselves compatible? – never mind, whether any wall of them can hope to be an adequate expression of the divine nature. There is far too little of the holiness and otherness of God or of the challenge to and escape from the power of sin. At times, it seems we are being urged to settle in and for suffering itself, rather than victory over suffering. It is no wonder Jesus is recorded as asking the man at the pool of Bethesda who had been there for thirty-eight years, whether he wanted to be healed. There may well be a security in illness and a strange comfort in suffering, which settles for the experience and context of suffering and does not look beyond it to the possibility of change, healing and transformation.

But this substitution of one set of conformity and dependency for another set, which is or are in themselves dubious, is paralleled in reflection on the motivation behind the talk of the weakness of God. In his critique of classical accounts of the immutability of God Moltmann describes the motives at work behind such a theology: 'Death, suffering and mortality must therefore be excluded from the divine being. Christian theology has adopted this concept of God from philosophical theology down to the present day, because in practice down to the present day Christian faith has taken into itself the religious need of finite, threatened and mortal man for security in a higher omnipotence and a Trinity' (*The Crucified God*, p. 214). But now there is a new motivating push. Today's faith 'must understand the deity of God from the event of the suffering and death of the Son of God and thus bring about a fundamental change in the orders of being of metaphysical thought and the value tables of religious feeling. It must think of the suffering of Christ as the power of God and the death of Christ as God's potentiality' (*ibid.*, p.215).

Bauckham makes a similar point as he reflects on the role of human suffering and the need for a theodicy which is adequate based on the idea of the crucified God (*Themelios* p. 12). The problem here is surely that another set of psychological needs and desires have simply been substituted for so-called inappropriate needs and desires. But by what criteria are either set more or less adequate? Such psychologically based motivation seems a dangerous basis for any expression of the nature of the eternal God.

Here again, we see the change of conformity to another set of philosophies, psychologies and ideologies. The need for change, the inadequacy of the traditional categories, the superiority of the alternatives and the evidence that such alternatives are not simply repeated the form of the mistakes of the past by substituting what is essentially a similar relationship, are all necessary to avoid the charge of being squeezed into the modern world's mould, without doing justice to God in and of himself.

Omission
Moltmann writes 'Because of his infinite passion, God takes upon himself the passion and death of Christ, so that we may become free and can live together for his glory. Through his suffering from us and his death for us, Christ has accepted us and brought us to be God's glory' (*The Power of the Powerless* p. 102). If God loves us so much that he is prepared to suffer for us, and from us and with us, then we too should at last be free – free for transformation. We do not have to hold fast to our image of ourselves or our own reputation. For we ourselves are

held fast and can no longer be lost. So we can unfold, and change (*ibid.*, p.103).

The obvious lack here is of any talk of the real point in the cross. It is to deal with the problem of sin. Sometimes it seems as if the mere fact of enduring suffering is in itself sufficient, and that suffering itself is then sufficient in itself to bring about transformation. But transformation from what? At a recent conference I heard a moving parallelism of significance between Paul's Galatian description of Christ redeeming us from the curse of the law by becoming a curse for us, for it is written 'Cursed is everyone who is hung on a tree' (Gal. 3:3), with death from a 'necklace' in South Africa. Does the how or the form of the death of Christ matter?

It does, for it is the shedding of innocent blood which brings about ransom, redemption, reconciliation, atonement. All of these imply a state before and after. Not a suffering and a coping with suffering, but a captivity to and in sin and a release from sin. The significance in the cross is the point of the cross. It is the victory of Christ over sin. It is the dealing of Christ with what William Still calls the root, the fruit and brute of sin. Talk of the cross and of the weakness of God seems strangely silent about its seriousness and its cure.

Part of the danger in talk of the weakness and suffering of God is a belittling of the reality of sin. It likewise leads to absence of reflection on the holiness of God and his refusal to look upon sin. It omits the power of God to overcome sin and transform the sinner.

The Gospel message to weak and suffering humanity offers genuine hope of change. But that transformation is essentially because sin – root, fruit and brute – has been dealt with. Moltmann says '(God) takes our handicaps on himself and makes them part of his own eternal life. He accepts our tears and makes them the expression of his own pain. This is how God heals all sicknesses and all griefs, by making every sickness and every grief his own suffering and his own grieving.

God accepts our life as it really is, and absorbs it into himself – only not the way we dream of, not our phantom life and our inhuman ideals. God accepts the whole of human nature in its infirmities, and heals it by communicating to it his eternal divine nature' (*The Power of the Powerless*, p. 147).

But it is not suffering itself which achieves any such end. It is only victory over sin. Simple identification with human suffering is not in and of itself transforming. It is not enough simply to get down in the gutter with humility. We needed to be lifted from the gutter of sin by the transforming victory of love over sin.

The charge is that talk of the weakness and suffering of God omits any consistent treatment of sin and the essence of transformation of human suffering in and through the cross because of the completed victory of Christ at Calvary.

Presuppositions and the Need for Change
It has already been suggested that the shift from building an account of God on Greek philosophical motives to modern political and psychological concepts may not be totally warranted. Those presuppositions may not be quite in need of the kind of change suggested and claimed.

Likewise, the notion that old-fashioned psychological needs must give way to the 'men and women come of age' psychological needs does not offer an escape from a reductionist psychological account and dependency for our expression of the reality of God.

Moltmann and Kitaman and others seem to suggest this is a pathway to a new grasp of theodicy, but fail to analyse where evil comes from and the total response of God in Christ to evil in not simply enduring suffering and death, but acting to overcome the sin which causes suffering and death. It is not enough to say that Christ, or God, suffers as we suffer and the cross reveals that identification with our suffering, for as in the case of temptation, Christ was tempted as we are yet without sin. He may or may not suffer as we do, but his suffering is surely of a different order – witness the cry of dereliction – and the point of that suffering gives full significance to it: victory over sin.

As Christ became obedient to death, he made himself helpless before those who would crucify him. Is that any basis for our own helplessness before suffering and evil in the world? But the weakness of Christ is not the same as our weakness, nor is it without radical results – *i.e.* redemption, reconciliation, ransom and atonement.

The presuppositions of this 'crucified God' theology must be questioned as must the embracing of certain presuppositions about what constitutes personhood, love and completeness. (*The Crucified God,* pp. 223-3).

We are offered a new set of presuppositions. But the burden of proof must be with the proponents of the new. They must show the inadequacy of all the old, the overwhelming need for the new, and the superior truth, adequacy and results of the new. Have all these been established?

Conclusion
The adequacy of the charges must be assessed, but it is possible to make some general conclusions.

Overdependency on current philosophies and ideologies is always a serious threat to the theological task, but we must avoid merely substituting today for yesterday and the problems of today's ideas of process, politics, psychology and anthropomorphisms for the problems of the past.

Moltmann in fact has uncovered again the problems we have with making sense of the incarnation and atonement. In such talk the danger is always of confusion of the persons within the Trinity and of making God too distant to transform or too near to make a difference to our human condition of sin. Both moves are essentially reductionist, but also form a challenge for more adequate expressions of incarnation and atonement.

Such theological writing likewise stresses the need for appropriate expressions of the nature of God. The total revelatory basis of theological epistemology and its grounding in ontology need to be made explicit. The content of the person of God in himself and in relationship with other members of the Trinity needs clarification. God's relation to evil and sin, especially in light of his holiness and glory, needs to be made clear and a proper understanding of the power of God in and through the work of Christ needs a more faithful treatment of Philippians 2 and of the Book of Revelation.

But in all this I have failed to confess the weakness of the church of God; to confess the continuing presence of sin and disobedience in ourselves as individuals and as a community; that the church in the world awaiting the final redemption of the body is still flawed by evil, the power of the Evil One, and the setting of the world, so it is as yet a bride without her bridal gown. The Gospel of grace is that God chooses the weak and the foolish, but that cannot mean that we are to seek weakness and foolishness, as if that would encourage or enable God to pick us. As with the glorious achievement of humility by trying to be humble, the flaw is that we cannot choose weakness. Or rather, we can, but it will not achieve the expected or desired result.

The church – we – are called to be the Bride of Christ. We are summoned to change, to be reliant on the power of God, who transforms us by the blood of the Lamb, and who fills us with the power of the Holy Spirit.

The reality of the weakness of the church drives us back to dependency on the reality of the power and grace of God. His grace is sufficient, for his strength is made perfect in our weakness.

IN DEFENCE OF *THE CRUCIFIED GOD*

RICHARD BAUCKHAM

This paper will focus on Moltmann's discussion of divine passibility in relation to the cross in *The Crucified God*, with some reference to his later work, but without attempting to cover the later discussions comprehensively. Since the best defence of a theologian is often a careful and sympathetic account of his views, the first part of the paper will concentrate on exposition and explanation of Moltmann's argument for divine passibility. In the second part of the paper, I shall set out a line of argument, different from but complementary to Moltmann's, which will in general support his view of divine passibility, but with some qualification.

I

(1) Three reasons for speaking of God's suffering

Although Moltmann does not explicitly set out these three as such, I think they can be identified in *The Crucified God* and Moltmann's subsequent treatments of the subject as three reasons – or perhaps it would be better to say, three elements in Moltmann's single reason for requiring Christian theology to speak of God's suffering. They are closely interconnected:

(a) *The Passion of Christ.* Only if we can say that God himself was involved in the suffering of Christ on the cross can we do justice to the place of the cross in Christian faith: 'How can Christian faith understand Christ's passion as being the revelation of God, if the deity cannot suffer?' (TKG 21).[1] To realise the full force of this

---

[1] In this paper the following abbreviations are used for Moltmann's works in English translation:

CG = *The Crucified God* (London: SCM Press, 1974)

argument, we must realise that in *The Crucified God* Moltmann was developing a theology of the cross in the sense of Luther's *theologia crucis* and explicitly as a modern continuation of the radical direction of Luther's *theologia crucis*. This makes the cross, in all of its stark negativity, the basis and criterion of Christian theology, 'the test of everything which deserves to be called Christian' (CG 7). In particular, it means that God is decisively revealed in the suffering and death of Jesus on the cross. The cross must be the criterion which distinguishes the Christian understanding of God from all others. Moltmann's criticism of the early church's understanding of the two natures of Christ, which distinguished the impassible divine nature from the passible human nature and attributed the suffering of Jesus only to the latter, is an application of this principle. The metaphysical concept of God which the Fathers took over from Greek philosophy defined the divine nature as the opposite of everything finite and made suffering and death axiomatically impossible for God. The two-natures Christology was a way of affirming the deity of the Christ who suffered and died, without redefining divine nature in the light of the cross. It understood divine nature in terms of a natural theology (*cf.* TKG 22) – in Luther's terms a *theologia gloriae* – which had no place for the cross, and then attempted to speak of the incarnation and the cross. The result could only be paradoxical talk of God suffering impassibly (TKG 22). In reality, Moltmann claims, the cross as the revelation of God is incompatible with the philosophical concept of the impassible God. If the cross is

---

CPS = *The Church in the Power of the Spirit* (London: SCM Press, 1977)

FC = *The Future of Creation* (London: SCM Press, 1979)

GC = *God in Creation* (London: SCM Press, 1985)

TKG = *The Trinity and the Kingdom of God* (London: SCM Press, 1981)

TTC = 'The "Crucified God": A Trinitarian Theology of the Cross,' *Interpretation* 26 (1972) 278–299.

found to contradict understandings of God derived from elsewhere, then the attempt must be made rigorously to understand the being of God from the event of the cross. It is in this sense that *The Crucified God* claims that taking seriously the theology of the cross calls for a 'revolution in the concept of God' (CG 4, 204):

> Within the Christian message of the cross of Christ, something new and strange has entered the metaphysical world. For this faith must understand the deity of God from the event of the suffering and death of the Son of God and thus bring about a fundamental change in the orders of being of metaphysical thought and the value tables of religious feeling (CG 215).

(b) *The Nature of Love.* Metaphysical theism has to eliminate from the notion of God's love for the world any element of reciprocity. God cannot be affected by the objects of his love. They can neither cause him pain nor increase his joy, which is perfect without them. Suffering, along with all feeling, cannot belong to God's love, which has to be understood rather as purely active benevolence: God's will and action for the good of his creation. Moltmann's approach is quite different: God's love is his 'passion' in the double sense of passionate concern (*Leidenschaft*) and suffering (*Leiden*). Love is not just activity on others but involvement with others in which one is moved and affected. Vulnerability to suffering is essential to it. The clash with the Greek concept is most apparent when Moltmann represents the Greek concept of God's inability to suffer as a deficiency rather than, as it was for Greek philosophy, a perfection:

> A God who cannot suffer is poorer than any man. For a God who is incapable of suffering is a being who cannot be involved. Suffering and injustice do not affect him.... But the one who cannot suffer cannot love either. So he is also a loveless being (CG 222).

Two important points need to be made about this argument from the nature of love. First, although we shall have to return to the question of anthropomorphism and analogy in speaking of divine and human love, it is evident that Moltmann is not simply saying that God's love must be like human love in every respect. Rather he claims that being affected by the beloved and therefore vulnerable to suffering is essential to what is best and most valuable in human love. *Pathos* is not a deficiency of human love, which must be stripped from our concept of divine love, but is rather love's greatness, without which it is not recognizably love.

Secondly, however, it is not strictly accurate to regard this argument as an argument from the nature of human love to the nature of God. In that case, it would be just another kind of natural theology, independent of the cross. Moltmann uses it in the context of a discussion of protest atheism's rebellion against metaphysical theism. It functions as no more than a negative demonstration that the apathetic god of metaphysical theism has nothing to offer the protest atheist who values his own human capacity to love and to suffer and to die (CG 222-3; *cf.* 253). It is not this argument, but the cross which reveals God's love to be suffering love. To say that God is love is to refer to the cross (TKG 82-83). Thus the argument about the nature of love is valid only in strict relation to the cross. Moltmann's point is that the only concept of God's love which can do justice to the cross is that of passionate concern which suffers from, with and for those it loves.

(c) *The problem of human suffering.* The theodicy question is the main context for Moltmann's discussion of the doctrine of God in chapter 6 of *The Crucified God.* The basic problem of traditional theism, with its purely active, impassible God, is the problem of theodicy: how can an all-powerful and invulnerable creator and ruler of the world be justified in the face of the enormity of human suffering? If such a God is not to function as a justification for innocent suffering, silencing all protest against it and inculcating meek submission to it as his will, then there must be rebellion against him in the name of goodness and righteousness. So metaphysical theism (to which Moltmann links the political theism which depicts God in the image of the absolute despot) has as its counterpart 'the only serious atheism' (CG 252), the atheism of protest, which Albert Camus describes as a 'metaphysical rebellion' (CG 221) against the God who sanctions suffering. So Moltmann, recognizing the justification of atheism's protest against the God of metaphysical theism on the ground of innocent suffering, seeks a way beyond both metaphysical theism and protest atheism, an understanding of God which neither suppresses nor evades the problem of suffering. He finds this in 'a theology of the cross which understands God as the suffering God in the suffering of Christ and which cries out with the godforsaken God, 'My God, why have you forsaken me?' For this theology, God and suffering are no longer contradictions, as in theism and atheism, but God's being is in suffering and the suffering is in God's being itself, because God is love' (CG 227).

Two points must be made also about this topic. First, once again, we should be cautious about regarding the problem of suffering as an argument for the suffering of God. The widespread modern Christian feeling that the loving God cannot be understood as remaining impassively aloof from the suffering of the world he loves is clearly shared by Moltmann, but he does not make this in itself an argument. In *The Crucified God* there is no discovery of the suffering God apart from the cross. The theodicy question, as sharpened by the impasse between theism and protest atheism, provides the context for fresh theological perception of the cross: 'Only when [Christian theology] has understood what took place between Jesus and his Father on the cross can it speak of the significance of this God for those who suffer and protest at the history of [suffering in] the world' (CG 227).

Secondly, it is important to recognize that the theodicy question is for Moltmann an aspect of soteriology as well as the primary contemporary context for the doctrine of God. In *The Crucified God* Moltmann understands the soteriological significance of the cross more broadly than it has usually been understood in the tradition, as including 'both the question of human guilt and man's liberation from it, and also the question of human suffering and man's redemption from it' (CG 134). Moltmann by no means underrates the former. In a later comment, having claimed that 'the universal significance of the crucified Christ is only really comprehended through the theodicy question,' he continues that, 'the interpretation of Christ's death on the cross as an atoning event in the framework of the question of human guilt is the central part of this universal significance; but it is not the whole of it, or its fullness' (TKG 52). In chapters 4 and 5 of *The Crucified God* he holds closely together the double soteriological significance of the cross: for justification and theodicy. Only in chapter 6 does the theodicy question become the dominant one, because it is so closely involved in the modern problematic of the doctrine of God. But it remains a soteriological issue: in other words, the point of relating God to suffering is not to explain suffering, but to redeem from suffering. Thus, although Moltmann in chapter 6 probes the theology of the cross as a question which goes beyond soteriology to the doctrine of God – the question of who God himself is in the event of the cross (and *cf.* FC 62-64) – the effect is not to detach the doctrine of God from soteriology but to relate the doctrine of God to soteriology. Just as Moltmann recognizes the soteriological interest in the patristic doctrine of the impassibility of God (CG 228, 267-9), so his interpretation of the cross as the event of God's suffering is strongly soteriological: all suffering becomes God's *so that he may overcome it* (CG 246). God's suffering is with those who suffer for the sake of their redemption from suffering.

Thus the three elements we have identified as contributing to Moltmann's need to speak of God's suffering are very closely connected: the cross reveals God to be love which suffers with and for those who suffer. Because God is love he is for himself (the doctrine of God) what he is for us (soteriology) in the event of his suffering love.

The three elements are probably the three major reasons why many other Christian theologians since the mid-nineteenth century have questioned the doctrine of divine impassibility.[2] But it is noteworthy that whereas the second and third have often been given independent validity, in Moltmann's *The Crucified God* they function not as independent reasons but only in the closest connexion with the first. Paul Fiddes's recent book on divine suffering[3] identifies these three as three major reasons why recent theology has come to speak of divine suffering, and adds a fourth: 'the world-picture of today,' by which he means the picture of the world as process and therefore of God as involved in the process and interacting with its freedom.[4] This idea of God's suffering the freedom he grants the non-human creation does later appear in Moltmann's doctrine of creation (GC 69, 210-11).

---

[2] See the survey in R. Bauckham, '"Only the suffering God can help": divine passibility in modern theology,' *Themelios* 9/3 (1984) 6-12, with bibliography.

[3] P.S. Fiddes, *The Creative Suffering of God* (Oxford: Clarendon Press, 1988) chap. 2.

[4] Fiddes, *Creative Suffering*, 37-45.

(2) Jesus' cry of dereliction as central to Moltmann's understanding of the suffering of God

Moltmann takes the words of Psalm 22, 'My God, my God, why have you forsaken me?,' spoken by the dying Jesus in Mark's account of the crucifixion (Mark 15:34), to be, though not as such a historical report of what Jesus said, an authentic interpretation of Jesus' dying cry which takes us closest to the theological reality of Jesus' dying and death (CG 146-7). The crucified Jesus' abandonment by God his Father is the deepest theological reality of the event of the cross and dictates the terms in which a theology of the cross must speak of God's suffering. It is worth noticing that a recent full study of the cry of dereliction, from both a biblical and a theological perspective, by the Italian theologian Gérard Rossé,[5] strongly supports the weight Moltmann gives to the cry and to a large extent, though with some qualifications, the significance Moltmann finds in it.[6]

In relation to the cry of dereliction we can take further what we have already said about soteriology and the doctrine of God. The cry has both dimensions. Its soteriological significance is Jesus' (and therefore God's) identification with the godless and the godforsaken in the depths of their abandonment. Here Moltmann makes a strong contemporary restatement of a traditional understanding of the cry.[7] But he is anxious to press beyond this to the cry's revelation of the significance the cross has for God himself. It is Jesus' cry to the Father who has abandoned him. Moreover, we do not take the incarnation seriously if we distinguish at this point

---

[5] G. Rossé, *The Cry of Jesus on the Cross*, tr. S.W. Arndt (New York: Paulist Press, 1987).

[6] Rossé denies that the cry expresses despair (*cf.* TKG 78-79) or rebellion (*cf.* CG 227): *Cry of Jesus*, 102, 108. He also questions the way Moltmann sees a real separation between the Father and the Son on the cross: *Cry of Jesus*, 136-138.

[7] For the history of interpretation, see Rossé, *Cry of Jesus*, chapter 5.

between the humanity of Jesus and the divine Son. In the relationship between Jesus and his Father on the cross, it is a question of 'the person of Jesus ... in its totality as the Son' (CG 207). Thus the cry of dereliction signifies an event of suffering between the Father and the Son, that is, in God himself: 'there God disputes with God; there God cries out to God; there God dies in God' (FC 65). This insistence on the cry of dereliction as having an inner-trinitarian significance which points to suffering in God is immensely important for understanding Moltmann's view of divine suffering. He wants to make clear that the cross is not just, as in traditional theology, an act of God external to himself for our salvation – an *opus trinitatis ad extra* – by which God in himself is unaffected. Rather, as an event in which the Son suffers abandonment by the Father, the cross is God acting in himself: 'But if God is acting in himself, then he is also suffering his own action in himself' (FC 65).

This is why Moltmann is not content with the way in which Chalcedonian Christology could speak of God's suffering and death, in terms of the doctrine of the two natures, nor even with the ways in which Rahner and Barth tried to take the traditional approach further (*cf.* CG 201-4; FC 62-64). However seriously these theologians had tried to attribute the suffering and death of the cross to God, it remained a matter of God's outward relationship to the world, not of his inner trinitarian relationships with himself. Moltmann takes the cry of dereliction to mean that the suffering of the cross affects God in his inner trinitarian relationships. This is why the soteriological approach to the cross is not enough. At this point, Moltmann tends to give the rather misleading impression that he is leaving soteriology behind in order to discuss an aspect of the cross (how it affects God) which is *not* of soteriological significance (*cf.* FC 62; CG 201). His tendency to separate, in discussion, what the cross means for God from what it means for us has some unfortunate consequences. But the separation, as we have already indicated, does not really mean that soteriology is left behind. Moltmann's point is rather that we do not understand the full soteriological significance of the cross until we have probed its significance for God himself. The depth and effectiveness of God's solidarity with the godforsaken are seen when it is realised that God suffers the godforsakenness of Jesus in himself. God's saving relationship to us takes place within and affects his trinitarian relationships to himself. The distinction between God in himself and God for us disappears (*cf.* FC 76).

(3) **The suffering of the cross as internal to the Trinity**
As Moltmann unpacks the meaning of the cry of dereliction, he describes a differentiated suffering of both the Father and the Son. That the Father and the Son both suffer, but in different ways, is essential to his location of the suffering of the cross in the relationship between the Father and the Son, and so within God, not just in the relationship between God and the world. It is not that only the incarnate Son suffers. Nor is it that the human Jesus suffers and God shares Jesus' experience of suffering by empathy.[8] Rather, while Jesus the Son suffers dying in abandonment by his Father, the Father suffers in grief the death of his Son. 'The grief of the Father is here as important as the death of the Son' (CG 243). In other words, Father and Son experience a mutual loss – the Son of his Father, the Father of his Son – but differently in that it is the Son who is left by the Father to die. Although Moltmann does not perhaps make this point as clear as he might, this mutual loss is the estrangement of godforsaken humanity from God taken, as it were, within the divine experience, through the Son's identification with the godforsaken, and suffered by God. But the nature of the suffering is peculiarly God's, since the mutual loss

---

[8] So, apparently, Fiddes, *Creative Suffering*, 168.

ruptures the unparalleled closeness of the Son and the Father.

Moltmann has been criticized for the way he divides the persons,[9] but to understand him we need also to appreciate the paradox he presents, according to which Father and Son are most deeply united precisely in their division. The event of the cross is the act of God's love for the world, in which Father and Son are united in a 'deep community of will' (CG 243). It is in their common love that the Father surrenders the Son to death and the Son surrenders himself to death. 'On the cross Jesus and his God and Father are divided as deeply as possible through an accursed death, and yet they are most deeply one through their surrender' (FC 73). It is this paradox which makes the cross salvific. God suffers the estrangement of sinful and suffering humanity from himself and includes it within the loving fellowship of his trinitarian being. Thus the Holy Spirit, the third trinitarian person, who unites the Father and Son in their love at the point of their most painful separation, is 'the creative love proceeding out of the Father's pain and the Son's self-surrender and coming to forsaken human beings in order to open to them a future for life' (TTC 294-5). In this way it is God's inner-trinitarian suffering which reaches the godless and the godforsaken with his love. The cross makes the human situation the situation of God, from which neither guilt nor suffering nor death can exclude anyone (CG 276-77).

(4) The cross as a unique event of divine suffering
Paul Fiddes rightly points out that one of the major tasks of a doctrine of divine suffering is to talk coherently of 'a God who suffers universally and yet is still present uniquely and decisively in the sufferings of Christ.'[10] He

---

[9] Rossé, *Cry of Jesus*, 136-138; Fiddes, *Creative Suffering*, 138-140, 202.

[10] Fiddes, *Creative Suffering*, 3.

finds Moltmann attempting to do this, but failing to do so satisfactorily.[11] In Moltmann's work after *The Crucified God* it is clear that he does not intend to confine God's suffering to the event of the cross (*cf.* CPS 62-64; TKG 118; GC 15-16, 69, 210-211). This is less clear in *The Crucified God* itself, but even there his discussion of Jewish theology – both Abraham Heschel's interpretation of the divine *pathos* in the theology of the Old Testament prophets and the rabbinic understanding of the *Shekinah* in the sufferings of Israel – requires that the God of Israel already suffered in his relationship with Israel (CG 270-74). Yet it is clear that Moltmann does not regard the cross as merely the revelation to us of the suffering God constantly experiences in his relation to his creation – a position which is found in some representatives of the English tradition of thought about divine passibility.[12] The cross, it seems, is unique not only for us but also for God. Even in Moltmann's later work, where he develops a much broader account of God's trinitarian history with the world from creation to consummation, the cross retains a unique and decisive place. If Moltmann is not fully successful in stating the character of this uniqueness, I think it can be interpreted in a way which does better justice to his thought than Fiddes' discussion of it.[13]

---

[11] Fiddes, *Creative Suffering*, 5-12.

[12] *E.g.* H.R. Rashdall, *The Idea of Atonement in Christian Theology* (London: Macmillan, 1919) 450-454; F. Young in J. Hick ed., *The Myth of God Incarnate* (London: SCM Press, 1977) 36-37.

[13] Fiddes, *Creative Suffering*, 9, misses the point: 'If God has always been really dwelling with people in their suffering, then he must have been having the same *kind* of experience which Moltmann attributes to the cross.' But this is to assume that God experiences the sufferings of Jesus only by empathy, as he does other sufferers' sufferings. This is Fiddes' own view (*cf. Creative Suffering*, 168, 260) but it is not Moltmann's, for whom Jesus' sufferings are experienced by God the Son, not as someone else's sufferings, but uniquely as his own human sufferings.

Not using Moltmann's words, one could say that the cross is the event in which God makes all human suffering his *own*. Here God does not merely enter by empathy into the suffering of all who suffer, but by an act of solidarity in suffering makes their suffering his own. In Moltmann's own words, God 'does not merely enter into [the human] situation of [godforsakenness]; he also accepts and adopts it himself, making it part of his own eternal life' (TKG 119). The differentiated suffering of Father and Son in the event of the cross, even if approached by God's suffering with Israel (CG 274; TKG 118), is unique, and essential to the cross as God's act of solidarity with the godless and the godforsaken. God the Son suffers abandonment *himself*, actually as one of the godforsaken; God the Father suffers the death of *his own* Son as one of the godforsaken. This understanding of the uniqueness of the cross of course requires the 'Alexandrian' type of Christology which Moltmann takes for granted (*cf.* TKG 118-19) – and of which Fiddes is critical from the point of view of his own more 'Antiochene' Christology.[14] But to be fully comprehensible it requires thought about the distinction, to which Moltmann gives no attention, between God's suffering *as God* and God's suffering *as human* (in the incarnation). We shall return to this point.

(5) The God-world relationship as reciprocal
Finally, we turn to the wider question of Moltmann's understanding of the relation between God and the world and its difference from the classical theistic understanding. The doctrine of divine impassibility was part and parcel of the view that God relates only actively to the world. Because he is complete in his own perfection in himself, he cannot be affected by the world, which would mean being changed by it. Moltmann, from *The Crucified God* onwards, develops, by contrast, a view of God's history with the world which is a history of reciprocal relationships. God's

---

[14] *Cf.* Fiddes, *Creative Suffering*, 138.

creation both causes him suffering and augments his joy. Moltmann calls this the trinitarian history of God, because, in conformity with the relationship of the Trinity to the cross which we have sketched, he sees God's relationship with the world taking place within the trinitarian relationships of Father, Son and Spirit. It is a relationship which really affects God because it is internal to his trinitarian self-relationship. God's changing relationships with his creation are at the same time changing relationships between the trinitarian persons. In experiencing the world God experiences himself differently. This idea is worked out in detail in *The Trinity and the Kingdom of God*.

However, the contrast with the classical view is not absolute, because Moltmann maintains a strong emphasis on the priority of God's voluntary love towards the world. It is only because God voluntarily opens himself in love to the world that he can be affected by it. This emerges, in the first place, in his criticism of the patristic doctrine of divine *apatheia*. Moltmann does recognize that the doctrine contained an important truth: that God is not *subjected* to suffering against his will *as creatures are* (CG 229-30). The Fathers made the mistake of recognizing only two alternatives:

either essential incapacity for suffering, or a fateful subjection to suffering. But there is a third form of suffering: active suffering – the voluntary laying oneself open to another and allowing oneself to be intimately affected by him; that is to say, the suffering of passionate love.... If [God] is capable of loving something else [than himself], then he lays himself open to the suffering which love for another brings him; and yet, by virtue of his love, he remains master of the pain that love causes him to suffer. God does not suffer out of deficiency of being, like created beings.... But he suffers from the love which is the superabundance and overflowing of his being (TKG 23; *cf.* CG 230).

It should also be noted that God's suffering is not only consequent on God's loving initiative. It also contributes to the fulfilment of God's loving purpose for his creation. God's suffering is powerful. It is a moment in his creative and redemptive activity. It is through his suffering that God liberates his creation for its participation in his eschatological joy (*cf.* TKG 59-60).

The notion of an important degree of reciprocity between God and the world (*cf.* TKG 98-99) has very broad effects on Moltmann's later theology, which we cannot fully explore here. The idea of divine suffering is increasingly subsumed under the broader notion of divine self-limitation or *kenosis*, as involved in the act of creation as such and as characteristic of all of God's relationships with his creation. Suffering in the sense of pain follows as a further step from suffering in the sense of allowing: God's letting creation be itself as other than himself and giving it a degree of freedom in relation to himself (*cf.* TKG 108-11, 118-19; GC 86-90). But Moltmann insists that this self-limitation in respect of God's omnipotence is at the same time a de-limitation in respect of his goodness (TKG 119; *cf.* GC 88-89). In other words, it enables his love to evoke the free response of his creation. It becomes clear that the issue of divine passibility is closely connected with the issue of divine and human freedom and their relationship, itself a major preoccupation in Moltmann's later work (*e.g.* TKG 52-60, 105-8, 191-222; GC 79-86).

II

Moltmann's understanding of the cross as an event of divine suffering contains valuable insights, but needs certainly some clarification and perhaps some qualification.

(1) The problem of patristic Christology

A discussion can usefully begin with the problem of patristic Christology, which, as Moltmann correctly sees, enshrined the contradiction which has always hampered the development of a thorough-going theology of the cross: 'since that time most theologians have simultaneously maintained the passion of Christ, God's Son, and the deity's essential incapacity for suffering – even though it was the price of having to talk paradoxically about "the sufferings of the God who cannot suffer." But in doing this they have simply added together Greek philosophy's "apathy" axiom and the central statements of the gospel. The contradiction remains – and remains unsatisfactory' (TKG 22).

From the point of view of the problem of divine suffering, patristic Christology had two rather different sides to it. On the one hand, it should be recognized that in Alexandrian Christology, as represented especially by Cyril of Alexandria, and in Chalcedonian orthodoxy, especially as clarified by the fifth ecumenical council, the Council of Constantinople of 553, it was very important to be able to say that God the *Logos* was the subject of the passion and death of Jesus. Such language was as old as Ignatius of Antioch, who spoke of 'the passion of my God,' and the paradoxes it engendered were equally traditional: Melito of Sardis (frg. 13) already writes, 'the invisible was seen..., the impassible suffered, the immortal died, the heavenly one was buried.' In the Alexandrian tradition a major concern in Christology became the need to maintain the single divine subject of the whole incarnate life, so that to be able to say that 'God was born' (and therefore Mary was 'Mother of God') and 'God suffered' were treated as the shibboleths of orthodoxy. The Antiochenes resisted such statements because they seemed to make divine nature passible, but the Alexandrians insisted on them because only in this way could the work of salvation be God's work. God the *Logos* must be the one and only subject of the whole of the incarnate life of Christ, including especially the redemptive passion and death. They allowed no human subject in Christ to whom such experiences could be attributed. That Chalcedon itself taught this Cyrilline doctrine of a single divine subject of the incarnation, to whom the suffering of Christ must be attributed, was not clear in the period immediately after Chalcedon, when its defence against the so-called Monophysites was in the hands of theologians who interpreted it in an Antiochene way, but its meaning was eventually clarified through the theopaschite controversy of the sixth century, in which the so-called Neo-Chalcedonians promoted a Cyrilline interpretation of Chalcedon, which was endorsed by the Council of Constantinople of 553. The significance of the theopaschite controversy has been undeservedly neglected by modern theologians who have tended to see Chalcedon as the conclusion of the patristic christological debate, so far as its relevance for later theology goes. Moltmann, who notes the controversy, incorrectly states that the theopaschite formula, 'One of the holy Trinity suffered in the flesh,' was rejected (CG 228).[15] In fact, it was endorsed by the Council of Constantinople, which maintained that 'Jesus Christ who was crucified in the flesh is true God and the Lord of glory and one of the Holy Trinity' (the statement alludes to 1 Corinthians 2:8 as the prooftext for saying that God was crucified). Such language was nothing new, but the Council established, probably quite correctly,[16] that Chalcedonian orthodoxy entailed it.

---

[15] Fiddes, *Creative Suffering*, 115 n. 11, says that 'while approved by the second Council of Constantinople in 553, it was finally rejected by the Western Church.' This is also incorrect.

[16] For the view that neo-Chalcedonianism was faithful to the intentions of Chalcedon, see P.T.R. Gray, *The Defence of Chalcedon in the East (451–553)* (Leiden: Brill, 1979).

Moltmann probably underestimates this side of patristic Christology,[17] but he correctly notes that the Fathers found it wellnigh impossible to see the suffering thus attributed to God as a real experience of suffering for God (CG 227-9). According to the doctrine of the two natures, also established at Chalcedon, God in the incarnation is the subject of two natures, his own impassible divine nature and the passible human nature he assumes in incarnation. To say that God suffered meant that he was the subject of the sufferings of his human nature. He who in his own divine nature is impassible suffered in his human nature. The Fathers might have resolved the paradox by saying that only in incarnation can God suffer, but in fact the axiom of divine impassibility was so strong that they usually resolved the paradox by minimizing the reality of the suffering for God. What Cyril seems to mean by the claim that God 'suffered impassibly' is that the *Logos* was aware of the sufferings of his human nature, accepted them as his own, because the human nature is his, but did not experience them as sufferings. No doubt this did not seem as docetic then as it does to us, because of the contemporary ideal of human detachment from suffering.[18] But it is logically unsatisfactory, because there can be no such thing as suffering unless *someone* actually suffers. Since Cyril denies a human subject in Christ, the crucifixion can be described as suffering only if God experiences it as suffering. He cannot simply acknowledge the suffering as his own without experiencing it as suffering, because unless he experiences it as suffering no suffering exists for him to own. In this sense the Antiochenes were correct: the only way to preserve the

---

[17] The discussion in CG 231-232 uses the term 'person' in a more Antiochene than Alexandrian-Chalcedonian way ('the whole of the divine and human person of Christ'), and so seems to miss the point that the *divine person* suffers and dies, though not in his divine nature.

[18] *Cf.* F.M. Young, 'A Reconsideration of Alexandrian Christology,' *Journal of Ecclesiastical History* 22 (1971) 103-14.

reality of Christ's human experience and the absolute impassibility of God was to attribute the former to the man Jesus, a human subject not identical with the *Logos*. Chalcedonian orthodoxy, with its single divine subject in Christ, must logically deny either that any suffering took place when Jesus was crucified or that God is absolutely impassible. But it would be quite coherent to claim that God can suffer *only* in incarnation, that is, only by experiencing the human experience of Jesus as his own.

(2) God's incarnate suffering

While it is true that the Fathers' Christology was hampered by their Platonic definition of divine nature, the problem raised by patristic Christology cannot be solved simply by rejecting their definition of divine nature, as Moltmann does. Taking incarnation seriously requires us to assert that divine nature – what it is for God to be God – includes the possibility of being human, that is, of making his own all the finite experience of a fully human life, of course without ceasing to be God. It is not possible to define divine nature in such a way as to exclude the properties of being human, as the Fathers did, and then unite the two natures, without separation or confusion, in the divine person of the *Logos*. Unless divine nature includes the possibility of being human, incarnation is not possible. But, on the other hand, incarnation does not mean a general dissolution of the difference between divine and human natures. Only in the unique instance of the man Jesus is God human in the full sense that he is all that it means to be a finite human creature. At this point, isolating the issue of suffering can be misleading. Whatever we may say about suffering, we are bound, if we take incarnation seriously, to distinguish between what can be said of God *as human* (in the incarnation) and what can be said of him *as God* (outside incarnation). Even if we took the most anthropomorphic language of the Old Testament as the criterion of what can be said of God, still many statements remain which can only be made of God as the subject of the human life of Jesus: that he eats, gets tired, sleeps, is afraid, dies. In fact, Moltmann's title makes just such a statement about God: that he was crucified. Precisely in order to preserve the reality of the incarnation, we must not abolish the difference between what is possible for God in incarnation and what is otherwise possible for God. In order to say that God suffered crucifixion, we need to be able to assert, not that some kinds of human experience have analogies in the divine experience, but that incarnation, which entails all the utterly and precisely human experience of a fully human life, is really possible for God. Then it follows that God suffered crucifixion in exactly the same way as it follows that God was suckled at Mary's breast and slept in a boat on the sea of Galilee.

I do not make this point in order to deny that God can suffer outside the incarnation. That question is still open. But it is important to be clear that, whatever may be said about God's suffering outside the incarnation, his human suffering as Jesus is unique, since this is precisely *human* suffering. There is a danger that a doctrine of divine passibility can promote its own peculiar kind of docetism. In other words, we may think of the suffering of Jesus as the kind of suffering which we suppose to be attributable to God, unconsciously reducing its fully human character and forgetting that the point of the doctrine of the incarnation is that in Jesus' case his utterly human suffering – his fear in Gethsemane, his loneliness as friends desert him, the excruciating physical agony, and so on – is precisely as utterly human suffering attributable to God. The inattentive reader of Moltmann's account of the cross as an event between the divine persons may succumb to this kind of docetism. It is not Moltmann's intention. What he wishes to say is that the thoroughly human history of Golgotha takes place within the relationships of the Trinity. But his general discussion of divine passibility, which does not distinguish God's suffering as human from his suffering as God, could mislead. We have noted Moltmann's admission that the doctrine of divine impassibility was legitimate insofar as it 'really says that God is not subjected to suffering in the same way as transient, created beings' (TKG 23). But applied too simply to God's suffering in Jesus this could seriously mislead. In Jesus God suffered precisely the sufferings of a transient, created being. Moltmann's statement applies to God's incarnate suffering only in the sense that in the act of incarnation God voluntarily assumed all the human experience of the man Jesus.

(3) God's non-incarnate suffering

In the incarnation God the Son suffers human suffering. Should we, with Moltmann, go on to say that in the event of the cross the Father also suffers, though differently? Three lines of argument may take us in that direction: (a) If incarnation is possible for God, then God is not limited by the traditional metaphysical attributes. (b) In the human life of the Son of God, the Father is revealed. But what is most revelatory of God in the human life of Jesus is his loving identification with the godless and the godforsaken by which he shares and suffers their fate. The supreme revelation of the Father's love is not a human example of purely active benevolence, but the *suffering* love of the crucified Jesus. So it is to this kind of love – love which through involvement with the beloved suffers – that we should consider God's love analogous. God's incarnate love in Jesus is of this kind because the incarnation is grounded in this kind of love in God. Of course, to speak of God's suffering love – other than in the incarnation – is to use anthropomorphic analogy. All personal language about God is anthropomorphic analogy. But this no more enables us to conclude that God does not really suffer than it enables us to conclude that God does not really love. The point is that whereas the tradition of metaphysical theism held that purely active benevolence was the only kind of human love which has an analogy in

God, the cross requires us to say that it is human suffering love to which God's love is analogous. Moltmann's claim that the Father suffers in grief the death of the Son on the cross is bold anthropomorphism, but consistent with much biblical language. As theology it may be criticized only if its analogical character is neglected and it is supposed to claim that we know what it was like for the Father to suffer the death of Jesus. Of course, we do not know what anything is like for God, only that some things in human experience have an analogy in divine experience. What does lay Moltmann open to the charge of speaking mythologically about the divine experience is his failure to distinguish, in his account of the cross as a trinitarian event, the human suffering of Jesus, which *is* human suffering, from the divine suffering of the Father, which is only analogous to human suffering. If we could speak as literally about the Father's experience as we can about the human experience of the incarnate Son, incarnation would not be necessary.

(c) The third line of argument is to take seriously the Old Testament revelation of God as the context for understanding the incarnation and the cross. Against the background of the Old Testament, the incarnation is in one sense something quite new, but in another sense continuous with the God of Israel's involvement with his people and their sufferings. Moltmann adumbrates this line of argument in his use of Abraham Heschel's pioneering study of the *pathos* of God in the prophets,[19] but it could be taken further with the aid of other studies in Old

---

[19] On Heschel, see Bauckham, '"Only the suffering God",' 9-10, and more fully: J.C. Merkle, 'Heschel's Theology of Divine Pathos,' in *Abraham Joshua Heschel: Exploring His Life and Thought*, ed. J.C. Merkle (New York: Macmillan/London: Collier Macmillan, 1985) 66–83; J.C. Merkle, *The Genesis of Faith: The Depth Theology of Abraham Joshua Heschel* (New York: Macmillan/London: Collier Macmillan, 1985) 130–135.

Testament theology,[20] such as Terence Fretheim's recent book on the suffering of God in the Old Testament.[21] Such studies not only show that the suffering of God is a far more pervasive theme in the Old Testament than the classic passages usually cited might indicate. They also take the Old Testament's anthropomorphic language about God seriously as revelatory of God, instead of dismissing as *mere* anthropomorphism not to be taken seriously, whatever does not accord with the traditional metaphysical concept of God.

One way of relating the Old Testament tradition of God's suffering to the cross as an event of divine suffering between the Father and the Son might be, in summary, as follows. God in the Old Testament suffers empathetically *with* his people in their sufferings. He also suffers grief *because* of his people when they reject him and are lost to him. Finally, both these kinds of suffering constitute a redemptive suffering *for* his people.[22] In Jesus God's identification with people in their sufferings reaches a new and absolute depth. He goes beyond empathy to an act of solidarity in which he suffers as one of the godless and the godforsaken, sharing their fate of abandonment. But this identification of God with those who suffer (in the person of the Son) at the same time causes him grief (in the person of the Father). In the Father's suffering of the death of Jesus God's grief at the loss of those who are estranged from him reaches a new and absolute depth. He suffers that loss as the loss of his own Son identified with

---

[20] *E.g.* E.S. Gerstenberger and W. Schrage, *Suffering*, tr. J.E. Steely (Nashville: Abingdon, 1980) 98-102; E. Jacob, 'Le Dieu souffrant, un thème théologique vétérotestamentaire,' *Zeitschrift für die alttestamentliche Wissenschaft* 95 (1983) 1–8.

[21] T.E. Fretheim, *The Suffering of God: An Old Testament Perspective* (Overtures to Biblical Theology 14; Philadelphia: Fortress, 1984).

[22] These three kinds of suffering of God in the Old Testament are distinguished and discussed by Fretheim, *Suffering of God*, chaps 7-9.

the godless and the godforsaken. Thus human estrangement from God comes between the Father and the Son, they suffer it in their common love for the world, and their mutual, but differentiated suffering overcomes the estrangement and so proves to be redemptive suffering for the world.

(4) Anthropomorphism and apophaticism

Finally, we return to what Moltmann calls metaphysical theism and offer a critique somewhat different from (though not contradictory to) Moltmann's. The tradition of metaphysical theism in Christian theology could be seen as having two rather different strands in it, both deriving from its origins in Platonism. The two strands may be called anthropomorphic[23] and apophatic. The first, dependent on the Platonic view that the human intellect is the element in human nature which is akin to the divine, conceives God as the supreme *Nous*. The human being is most akin to God when the mind, which is the true self, abstracted from the body and all relations with the material world, contemplates eternal, unchanging truth. God is 'without body, parts or passions,' as in the Platonic view the human mind can be when it recollects its true nature. Divine *apatheia*, therefore, is not so much a definition of God as wholly other than us, but rather the ideal to which Platonic humanity itself aspires. For this view of God as the supreme Mind, to attribute knowledge and will to God is appropriate, if analogical, but to attribute emotion or bodily sensation to God is inappropriate. The latter is considered anthropomorphic, the former not. In reality, of course, this view is selective anthropomorphism. It speaks of God in terms of one facet of human personality (impassive reason), not of others, and corresponds to an

---

[23] I use the term 'anthropomorphic' in the general sense of applying to God language which we otherwise use of human persons, not merely in the sense of attributing the physical features of human persons to God.

anthropology which treated this facet as the highest element of human nature. Biblical anthropomorphism is also selective, but not in this way. The biblical God does not, for example, eat, sleep, fear, doubt or die, but he is, for example, grieved and roused to anger, he desires and feels compassion, he hides his face and shows strength with his arm, just as much as he knows and wills. The deep-rooted prejudice that reference to God's reason and will is more literal than reference to God in emotional and physical terms derives from Platonism, rather than the Bible. It would be better to recognize that all personal language about God is equally anthropomorphic. Such language should be justified not by a Platonic anthropology in which the human mind is the image of God, but by a biblical anthropology in which human personality as a psychosomatic whole and in community is the image of God.

The second strand in the tradition of metaphysical theism is negative theology. It does not tell us what God is like (he is the supreme intellect) but what he is not (he is not finite like us). All the traditional metaphysical attributes can be understood in this sense: God is not limited by time as we are, God is not limited by space as we are, God is not limited in knowledge or power as we are, God is not subject to change or suffering as finite creatures are. God transcends finite existence in every respect: this is all the metaphysical attributes really tell us about God. In Platonism, this kind of negative theology gave God a transcendence which removed him from all relationship with the world: the metaphysical attributes exclude their finite opposites and make it impossible for God to relate to this world. The great struggle of patristic theology was to recognize God's transcendence as the wholly other whose incomparable difference from creation does not exclude but enables his incomparably intimate relationship with his creation, in immanence and incarnation. Probably the most effective way of continuing that struggle is to understand the metaphysical attributes not as excluding but as including their opposites.[24] That God transcends time need not mean that he cannot also relate to us in time. That God transcends space need not mean that he cannot also relate to us in space. That God is not subject to change or suffering as we are need not mean that he cannot change or suffer in any way at all. That God transcends every human limitation need not prevent him also assuming every human limitation in incarnation.

To speak as adequately as we can of God we need to use both anthropomorphic and negative language, but not to confuse the two.[25] Negative theology should not inhibit the use of anthropomorphism, but stands as a permanent qualification of all anthropomorphism. God suffers, but as the one who transcends all finite suffering. We may say that there is something analogous to human suffering in the divine experience, but we may not thereby claim that we know what it is like for God to suffer. We might even say, with Cyril, that God suffers impassibly, but not, as he did, of the incarnation. The incarnation, in which God is not like us but actually one of us, anchors all our language of God in his concrete human history. But the ocean in which it floats is the boundless mystery of God's infinity.

---

[24] Cf. H. Küng's notion of the 'dialectic of the attributes': *The Incarnation of God*, tr. J.R. Stephenson (Edinburgh: T. & T. Clark, 1987) 445–453.

[25] On this, cf. S. Tugwell, 'Spirituality and Negative Theology,' *New Blackfriars* 68 (1987) 257–263.

THE IMPOSSIBILITY OF DIVINE PASSIBILITY

PAUL HELM

> There is but one only living and true God, who is
> infinite in being and perfection, a most pure spirit,
> invisible, without body, parts, or passions,
> immutable....
>
> *Westminster Confession of Faith* II.1

My aim in this paper is to attempt three things; to provide
a definition of divine impassibility, to defend this as a
central, and therefore Scriptural tenet of Christian theism,
and lastly to make some brief remarks in defence of the
religious adequacy of the concept of divine impassibility.

I

Firstly, then, a concept of divine impassibility. An
understanding of this is, in my view, best approached
through an understanding of divine immutability. In fact,
impassibility is entailed by immutability in the strong
sense of that term that (I shall argue) is required in the
case of God. And immutability in that strong sense is in
turn entailed by divine timeless eternity. So a simple way
to establish divine impassibility would be to argue:

(1) God is timelessly eternal.

(2) Whatever is timelessly eternal is unchangeable.

(3) Whatever is unchangeable is impassible.

(4) Therefore, God is impassible.

For certain purposes this argument is perfectly
satisfactory; however, arguing in this way does not
succeed in throwing much light on the notion of

119

impassibility. And unless that notion can be made initially plausible, then it is open to anyone to counter-argue that since it is doubtful that God is impassible he is neither unchangeable nor timelessly eternal. And so for these reasons if for no other I wish to spend a little time trying to elucidate the notion of impassibility and defending it in its own terms.

Both immutability and impassibility are *modal* terms; that is, each refers to not merely to what is or is not so, but to what can and cannot be so. It is not simply that an impassible X is not affected in a certain way; it *cannot* be affected at all. Impassibility and immutability, if true of God, refer to divine inabilities; God cannot change or be changed, and *a fortiori* God cannot be changed by being affected. So that impassibility is a kind of immutability.

Not every kind of change is ruled out by immutability or impassibility; suppose, on thinking of him, a person comes to fear or rejoice in God. Something is true of God now that was not true of him before, namely that God is now feared by that person. So, in a sense, God has changed from not being feared to being feared. But, as one quickly realises, the change is not 'in' God but 'in' one of his creatures who has now come to fear God. This distinction between a 'real' change and one that is a mere relational change is hard to make precise, but that there is such a distinction is obvious.

Furthermore, the kind of change ruled out by impassibility is ruled out on logical grounds. George Washington is reputed to have said 'Father, I cannot tell a lie, I did it with my little hatchet'. But God does not find it impossible to change as George Washington found it impossible to tell a lie, nor is it merely impossible for God to change because he has chosen or promised not to change, but it is logically inconceivable that God might change; there are no possible worlds in which God is really changed by the actions or omissions of his creatures, or by any real change in the universe that he has created.

So far I have understood impassibility rather schematically, in terms of the impossibility of certain sorts of change in God. An attempt will now be made to spell out the idea of impassibility a little further, being helped in this by Richard Creel's excellent discussion[1] of the definitions of impassibility.

In the first chapter of *Divine Impassibility* Creel provides a helpful survey of definitions of impassibility, the core one of which is that A is impassible if A cannot be affected by any outside force[2]. Creel then goes on to consider the possible respects in which an individual might be impassible in this sense; impassible in his nature, his will, his knowledge and his feelings. Clearly an individual who is impassible in the sense defined in each of these respects is impassible to the highest degree.

God is impassible in his nature. The fact that God has a nature, the fact that he has certain properties *essentially*, in every possible world in which he exists, does not entail impassibility; for the simple reason that those properties might be such that though God has them essentially, they are such that they change over time. To say that God is impassible in his nature is to say that his nature is such that none of the properties that comprise it are such that they can change or be changed.

Further, God is impassible in his will. His will cannot change or be changed. Although it is not part of my claim that any of these theses can be established by reason alone, nevertheless the impassibility of the divine will could be said to follow logically from divine omniscience

---

1 *Divine Impassibility*, Cambridge, 1986
2 Creel *op. cit.* p. 9

and omnipotence. For if God knows everything, he can have no reason to change his will. God does not have to wait and see in order to do. And if he is omnipotent no-one can be sufficiently powerful to make him change his will.

God's will is best understood not as an act, a volition, or as a series of volitions, but as an eternal, fully-informed disposition which, when faced with the knowledge of certain creaturely actions, invariably acts in a way that is appropriate to that action (given the divine purpose), and so appears to the creature to *react*. Each divine moral attribute may be thought of as operating within a field; in any change in the creature appropriate to that field, the attribute in question is experienced as a *change*.

Creel argues[3] that God's knowledge of creaturely change involves him in change; for he comes to know that A is happening and then that B is happening, as we do. Clearly I must deny this, as I have previously argued for God's immutability and eternity. The price for doing so (there is no such thing as a free argument!) is to deny certain kinds of knowledge to God, the knowledge of change. Does God change? No – he 'merely' changes from the point of view of those in time. There is a large literature on this point, and I do not propose to go over that well-traversed ground again here.

Further, Creel says that while God does not know what will happen, he knows (from his knowledge of the total array of possibilities) what he will do if and when each one of these possibilities is actualised. But this appears to be a denial of omniscience (of the Scriptural claim that God knows the end from the beginning), and also to require God to change in certain ways.

---

[3] Creel *op. cit.* p. 205

So far we have considered the impassibility of God's nature, of his will and of his knowledge. But to some the central issue has not yet been addressed. According to the concept of divine impassibility it may seem that God is without feeling. The short answer is: No, God is supremely blissful. But this requires a little amplification.

The idea of impassibility, if true of God, appears at first sight to impoverish rather than to enrich him. Surely a God who is incapable of being affected by his creatures is a cold, unsympathetic[4] God who is unworthy of worship, and who is certainly not the God of Scripture. I will try to deal with the Scripturalness or otherwise of this doctrine later. But what of the first charge?

'Feeling' is an ambiguous term. I may have a feeling of numbness in my leg as well as a feeling of depression that the numbness betokens the onset of Parkinson's Disease. The first kind of feeling is only possible for those individuals who have bodies with appropriate nervous systems. It is feeling in the sensory sense. Christological considerations apart (which are happily not my concern in this paper), I take it that no one wishes seriously to ascribe bodily feelings to the eternal God. But in the same way that it makes no sense to ascribe bodily feelings to God, because God is not that sort of being, so, the doctrine of divine impassibility asserts, it makes no sense to ascribe emotional affects to God because he is not that sort of being.

Take the following picture; that of an individual who though capable of expressing emotion, never in fact expresses it, or (bearing in mind the earlier discussion)

---

[4] The matter of divine sympathy (in connection with divine timeless eternity) is discussed by Murray MacBeath and Paul Helm, 'Omniscience and Eternity' *Proceedings of the Aristotelian Society, Supplementary Volume* LXIII, (London, 1989) pp. 55–87

who never *can* express it. This seems to be the paradigm case of an insensitive or completely withdrawn personality of the sort that is sometimes to be found in psychiatric institutions. Is it not blasphemous to suppose that God is like this?

Of course it is blasphemous. But this is not because God is capable of being emotionally affected, but for an altogether different reason.

The picture of the withdrawn or insensitive person is based on the distinction with which we are familiar, that between a disposition and the exercise of that disposition. A person may be disposed to be angry, or fearful or joyful; under certain circumstances or conditions he may express one or other of these emotions; when he is frightened then, other things being equal (for instance, he does not have an overriding reason for inhibiting the expression of his emotion), he expresses his fear. And even if he does not express his fear he may nonetheless be fearful, feel fearful. A person who either lacked the disposition to be fearful, or having the disposition could never exercise it (if this makes sense) is rightly regarded as an impoverished individual; someone to be pitied and helped rather than to be admired or emulated.

If we were to transfer this distinction between a disposition and its exercise to God, then it would become appropriate to expect occasions when the disposition is exercised as the relations in which God exists towards his creatures change and develop. God has the disposition to love; as he becomes aware of need, his disposition to love comes into exercise; he is affected by the need of his creatures; as the need vanishes, the disposition is no longer exercised.

But this is altogether the wrong way of thinking about the character of God; for it supposes that there are occasions when God is less than wholly active, and moreover that these are the typical conditions of his existence. So that while it may be helpful to think of God's moral attributes as dispositions, in that they have the stability and uniformity that dispositions in general have, unlike human dispositions they are dispositions that are always/eternally exercised. They are maximally active; that is, there is no actual situation in which God requires to exercise a given disposition in which that disposition is not exercised, every disposition that comprises the divine character is exercised, and each is exercised without any limitation or conditionality. So that, for example, the love of God is never not exercised where it is appropriate for it to be exercised.

To say that God is without passions is not to say that he is quite amoral. To us such notions as commitment and intense concern are strongly associated with feeling, and with the capacity to react to situations in appropriate ways. But this is most definitely not the case in God, but rather the opposite conclusion should be drawn, that it is because God's character is both essential to him and never dispositional (in the sense in which creatures have dispositions *i.e.* have traits that may not be exercised) that it is mistaken to think of him as having passions, affects. This is part of what the scholastics and others have meant when they have referred to God as 'pure act'. There is no unfulfilled potential in God, and an unexercised disposition is of course just that.

G.L. Prestige put these points rather well, in discussing the view of the Apostolic Fathers on divine impassibility:

It is clear that impassibility means not that God is inactive or uninterested, nor that He surveys existence with Epicurean impassivity from the shelter of a metaphysical insulation, but that His will is determined from within instead of being swayed from without. It safeguards the truth that the impulse alike in providential order and in redemption and sanctification comes from the will of God. If it were possible to admit that the impulse was wrung from Him either by the needs or by the claims of His creation, and that thus whether by pity or by justice His hand was forced, He could no longer be represented as absolute; He would be dependent on the created universe and thus at best only in possession of concurrent power.[5]

Aquinas, for example, does not object to some of what are affections in human beings being a part of God's character,[6] he only objects to those affections which, if they are had by anything, require that individual to be passive and to be in time. So that if there are attributes which, though they in fact carry such implications when possessed by human beings, do not when possessed by God, then Aquinas is ready to recognise the possibility of such in God. And clearly there are such – love, joy, delight, care and grace, for example. God has each of these with the greatest possible intensity and power.

Bringing all this together, perhaps we could approach a definition of divine impassibility as follows: first, a definition of 'disposition', then a claim that God has an essential character which cannot be dispositional in the sense defined, *i.e.* for any moral trait that God has (and which of course he has essentially) that trait cannot be dispositional. So, God is impassibly X (where X is any (appropriate) disposition of God (for example, joy)) only if:

(i) God has X essentially

(ii) X is necessarily maximally exercised.

---

[5] *God in Patristic Thought* (London, 1956) p. 7.
[6] *Summa Contra Gentiles* I.90

In using the word 'impassibility' some may intend to focus not on emotional change, but on change by emotion. Emotion is here considered not as what changes, but as what is the source of other changes. Then a definition of impassibility would be something like: A is impassible if and only if it is logically impossible for any of A's beliefs or intentions to be changed by emotional factors. This is not so much a definition of a different concept of impassibility as a consequence of the definition just given, since if an individual cannot be changed then *a fortiori* he cannot be changed by emotion.

II

At first sight it seems to be a daunting task to defend divine impassibility from Scripture, because much of the Scriptural language about God is activistic in character. God is portrayed as someone who is, for example, angry, who repents, who laughs, who has people in derision, who takes delight in – the traits of a person with a rich emotional life. To defend the impassibility of God would appear both to be dauntingly impossible and unnecessary, a sort of theological revisionism of a thoroughly unappetising kind.

Of course while God is portrayed in Scripture as having emotions he is not said to have just any emotion; he is not, as far as I am aware, ever said in Scripture to be, for example, agitated, tormented, melancholy, harassed, anguished, homesick, nostalgic, distressed, tormented, bitter, dismayed, enraged, euphoric, enraptured, anxious, hysterical, genial or despondent. The range of emotion ascribable to God must, for the Christian, be derived inductively from Scripture.

Nevertheless, to suppose that the impassibility of God is to be rejected because it rides roughshod over much biblical data would be too hasty a reaction. For God is also portrayed in Scripture as having a body – ears, a nose, back parts, a mouth, and so on. No one would rush to draw the conclusion that because God is portrayed in Scripture as having a body, that therefore he has one. The presence of anthropomorphism is standardly recognised in all biblical interpretation. Why then not anthropopathism?

One argument why not might be: because while God's possessing an ear, say, is incompatible with his being spiritual and incorporeal in nature, his being angry, or his repenting, is not. Harking back to our earlier distinction, it might be said that nothing without a body can feel a sensation in his ear, but a disembodied mind can feel emotions. At least, it would appear to require argument to show that this is not the case, and this fact alone appears to put a difference between having a body and having emotions.

Nevertheless, there are deeper reasons for rejecting divine passibility than those that concern real or supposed parallels between having an ear and having a spasm of anger. These reasons have to do with the fact that there are two sets of data in Scripture about God; namely those data which portray him as having traits that are compatible with him being human, and those that are incompatible with humanity. The former have already been mentioned; what are the other? All those data portraying God as infinite and timelessly eternal; as the Creator of all that is; as immutable.

Faced with these data, how is one to proceed in constructing a doctrine of God from Scripture? Which of these inconsistent or incompatible sets of data takes priority? Which data control the remainder? There are two alternatives. One would be to say that the anthropomorphic and anthropopathic data are logically prior to any other. As a consequence God has a body, a physical location in heaven, and a rich ever-changing emotional life. And as a consequence of this the language ascribing eternity and immutability to God must be taken by the theologian as hyperbolic; to ascribe eternity to God is then exactly like ascribing it to the time that stands still for us while we wait in the dentist's waiting room, or like the lover who says of his beloved that her face is divine.[7]

The alternative is to say that statements of the infinity, the eternity and immutability of God, and of his omniscience and omnipotence, take priority and that the other language of Scripture about God is strictly *a d hominem*. This seems to be the only alternative; it does not seem to be feasible to distinguish between body-language and passion-language and to classify the former as *ad hominem* and the latter, along with eternity and immutability, as the literal truth about God. Indeed, as we have seen, it is logically impossible to do this, since immutability is incompatible with the changefulness that the onset of a passion requires.

So there is a straight choice. Put in such a stark way it seems obvious – obvious to me, at least – what that choice should be. The metaphysical or ontological or strictly literal data must control the anthropomorphic and anthropopathic data, and not *vice-versa*. The alternative is quite unacceptable, namely, a theological reductionism in which God is distilled to human proportions. But worse than that. For anyone who says that such a reduction is correct immediately has another decision to make. Not only is there an abundance of anthropomorphic and anthropopathic data about God in Scripture, there is data

---

[7] For an example of a philosopher who appears to treat such language as hyperbolic, see O.K. Bouwsma 'Anselm's Argument' in *The Nature of Philosophical Inquiry* ed. Joseph Bobik (Notre Dame, 1970) pp. 252–293. In a similar way if the language of passion simply indicates moral intensity there is no problem.

which ascribes to him the properties of animals and physical objects; he is a rock, a tower, he roars like a lion, and so on. So either the reduction must continue until it includes such concepts, or it ought never to have been started in the first place.

Given the view that the metaphysical or ontological or strictly literal data control all other, it seems to be sufficient for establishing the impassibility of God that one can establish his timeless eternity and immutability, for passibility is a species of change, and if God is unchangeable then *a fortiori* he cannot change by being emotionally affected.

Given the hermeneutical assumptions or principles outlined above, the timeless eternity and immutability of God could be established from texts such as 1 Samuel 15:29; Psalm 90; Psalm 102:27; Malachi 3:6; Isaiah 41:4; John 17:24; Romans 11:29; Timothy 1:9; 6:16; Hebrews 1:10–12; James 1:17; Revelation 4:8–10.

However, as noted earlier, this is a rather indirect defence of impassibility. Is there a more positive set of reasons why, independently of the fact that impassibility is entailed by immutability, it should be accepted by the Christian theologian?

Since there is nothing morally wrong or intellectually incoherent with emotional change *per se*, the reason for not ascribing it to God must be that it is incompatible with other, more deeply entrenched (in terms of the biblical data) divine attributes or powers.

Earlier a distinction was made between that meaning of impassibility which is incompatible with the change that emotion brings, and that which is incompatible with emotional change *per se*. In the case of the first, one clear reason for not ascribing such emotion or passion to God is that it is incompatible with his rationality and wisdom. To act upon emotion or passion is to act when the judgment is in abeyance. Emotion clouds the judgment, or functions in place of the judgment. In any case, God is never portrayed in these terms in Scripture.

There are, however, certain emotions ascribed to God in Scripture which may imply ignorance; for example surprise and astonishment. The most notable one is repentance, not simply in the strict sense of a change in mind (which may not have any implications for emotion), but with emotional accompaniments of contrition and regret. God is frequently said to repent (e.g. Gen. 6:6; Ex. 32:14; 2 Kings 20:1–5; Jonah 3:4–10; Isa. 38:1–5; Jn. 3:10). And, in at least one celebrated case, God is even said to have changed his mind when he was asked the second time, after having refused to change his mind when asked the first time (the case of Hezekiah, Isaiah 38). The fact that these emotions imply ignorance is a conclusive reason for thinking that they cannot be attributed literally to God.

In a parallel way, certain other emotions ascribed to God imply a deficiency in his power, particularly those emotions which portray God as being overcome. For these reasons, the language of emotional change, when ascribed to God in Scripture, must be regarded as anthropopathic.

Why, then, if the biblical language which portrays God as having emotions cannot be literally true, is it employed in Scripture? No better general answer has been given to this question, to my mind, than the one that is found throughout the writings of John Calvin; namely, that God accommodates himself to human limitations, he condescends to human incapacity and weakness in allowing such terms to be ascribed to him, and, more to the point, in ascribing such terms to himself.[8]

This seems to be a good general explanation, for two interconnected reasons. The first is that it preserves the proper sense of direction. The language of accommodation is not the outcome of the striving of the human mind to make something out of God, but is expressive of an act (or acts) of divine condescension. The movement of direction is from God to mankind, and not *vice-versa*. Furthermore, being an act of accommodation, it is an act of grace, and as such is congruent with God's revelation of grace in Christ, and with the whole idea of revelation as the disclosure of what would otherwise be unfathomable. Divine revelation is evangelical both in content and in motive.

It may seem from what Calvin says that divine accommodation is a mere teaching tool, a concession to those of weak capacity, as thinkers as different as Philo and Locke maintained. But behind what may seem merely a psychological or epistemological economy on God's part there lies a logical point of some importance.

Calvin's claim is not that we will not understand God at all unless he condescends to speak to us in human-like and activistic ways; for there is much in Calvin to show that he held the exact opposite. The very fact that we know certain expressions to be divine accommodations implies that it is possible to think of God in non-accommodated ways. It would be wrong to read into Calvin the theological agnosticism of much post-Kantian Protestant theology.

---

[8] And not only Calvin. For example, Clement of Alexandria, according to Prestige, makes the point that 'deity cannot be described as it really is, but only as human beings, themselves fettered to the flesh, are capable of hearing; the prophets therefore adopted the language of anthropomorphism as saving concession to the weakness of human understanding' (*op. cit.* p. 8).

Kant claimed that all human knowledge of the external world takes place under the categories of space and time. The human mind is so structured that to suppose that something might be known about what existed beyond these boundaries is simply to generate antinomies, patterns of thought which are apparently contradictory. Kant is here making a general philosophical claim about whatever is to count as human knowledge. One well-known consequence of this position is that Kant is agnostic about the nature of God, since God is outside space and time; Kant proceeds to construct or reconstruct a doctrine of God in wholly moral terms, a God who is the source of morality, the postulate of the pure practical reason, but about whom nothing more can be known.

It is natural, and tempting, to read the Calvinistic doctrine of divine accommodation in Kantian terms, but mistaken to do so. Mistaken because Calvin is not an agnostic or a reductionist about the nature of God, for he believes that God has revealed much about his nature in Scripture, less so in nature. And mistaken also because, as a consequence of this first position, Calvin does not think that it is a necessary feature of the human mind that it cannot understand what falls outside the boundaries of space and time.

The reason for divine accommodation, as far as Calvin is concerned, is at first blush much more pragmatic and functional than that. It is that given that God has acted in history, even though such actions are the result of his eternal decree, they are best understood and responded to when understood as the actions of a person who is himself in time. But the reason for accommodation is not only pragmatic and functional. Once again, the centrality of God's grace in the activistic language of Scripture needs to be given emphasis. It is because God wishes people to respond to him that he *must* represent himself to them as one to whom response is possible, as one who acts in time. Only on such an understanding is that divine-human interaction which is at the heart of biblical religion possible.

So at the heart of Calvin's doctrine of accommodation is a logical point; namely, that it is a logically necessary condition of dialogue between people that those people should act and react in time. Impassibility has priority because it is an essential property of God, whereas his creating a universe in which there are creatures with whom he converses is a contingent matter. Nevertheless if that dialogue is to be real and not make-believe, then God cannot represent himself as wholly impassible, for then dialogue would be impossible.

So there is a metaphysical or ontological doctrine of God portrayed in Scripture; and where the language of God is non-metaphysical *i.e.* is anthropomorphic or anthropopathic, the reason for this is, broadly speaking, both pragmatic and logical, the need to represent God to men in ways which do not pander to the natural (*i.e.* sinful) torpor and sluggishness of human mind, but also the need for God to reveal himself in such a way as to make dialogue between himself and his human creatures possible.

III

To this view of divine impassibility a number of important objections have been put; namely, that to understand the biblical God as one who is timelessly eternal, immutable, omniscient and omnipotent, is in fact to allow the poison of categories of Greek thought to adulterate the pure milk of the word of God; and that such an account ignores or devalues the 'activistic' language of numerous biblical passages. Let us consider each of these objections in turn.

First, then, the charge that the whole metaphysical scheme of which impassibility is a part represents the intrusion of Greek thought into biblical language.

One argument against this view, is that biblical language and metaphysical concepts (whether these concepts are derived from Greek sources or from elsewhere) are not strict rivals. This is because of the fact that from the point of view of metaphysics the Bible is an underdeveloped book; there are few, if any, passages which are theoretical and reflective, or which make general claims and which rebut alternatives, of the sort typically advanced in metaphysical discussion. So the Bible does not repudiate developed metaphysics; rather, for the most part it obliquely sidesteps it, for its interests are for the most part elsewhere. But this does not mean that its first-order statements do not have metaphysical implications, only that they are not themselves metaphysical claims.[9]

While the categories of Greek philosophy, or for that matter Cartesian or Kantian philosophy, might be the *occasion* for maintaining some metaphysical view from Scripture, they are not (or ought not to be) the *grounds* or *reason* for maintaining, say, divine impassibility or immutability. Greek or some other philosophy might provide the conceptual tools for developing the doctrine of divine impassibility, but it does not follow that what doctrine results is derived not from Scripture but from philosophy.

To show this, it is sufficient to cite cases where Greek metaphysical doctrine is denied in the interests of being faithful to the biblical witness. A noteworthy case is the medievals' refusal to take from Aristotle the doctrine of

---

[9] For further comment on this, see Paul Helm, *Eternal God* (Oxford, 1988) Ch. 1.

135

the eternity of matter in the interests of maintaining the biblical doctrine of divine *creation ex nihilo*. Creel[10] cites another instance; Aristotle's God lacked all emotions, but this is not entailed by divine impassibility as understood in classical Christian theism, as we have already noted.

Another reason for being sceptical of this suspicion of Greek philosophy is as follows: many of the metaphysical propositions of the various Greek thinkers present, like any other thought that is intelligible and consistent, certain logical possibilities. We might say that Greek thought drew many such possibilities to human attention for the first time. For example from Greek thought we have derived the idea of something's existing timelessly eternally. Once this idea surfaces, the question may be raised by the Christian thinker, 'Does God exist timelessly eternally?'

There are only two possible answers to this question; either he does, or he does not. The reason for believing that he does, or that he does not (whichever the case may be) must be derived from the Scriptural data. But the knowledge of the possibilities themselves may derive from Greek philosophy, science fiction, *The Lord of the Rings* or anywhere else. While sources such as these might present certain abstract possibilities, it is for the biblical theologian to check the extent to which these might be adopted wholesale, or in a modified form, by anyone who wishes to present the biblical data in a summative, consistent and coherent form.

Much as one may like to, one cannot avoid metaphysics by taking refuge in divine passibility even though one suspects that there is a strong anti-metaphysical bias at work in those who favour it. To see this, one only needs to consider the questions: is God's passibility essential to

---

[10] Creel *op. cit.* p.10.

him or not? Is his being passible essential to him at all times in his life? He has suffered once; could he suffer again? Could he be overcome once the redeemed are in heaven? The passibilist may not be able to answer these questions but there is no denying either that they can be asked or that they are as Greek-sounding as the corresponding questions addressed to the impassibilist.

It is the continuous, repeated checking of any idea against the biblical data which is the only safeguard against rationalism, against an *a priori* treatment of the text, whether that treatment derives from philosophy or from some other source. It is the only safe method; this does not mean that such a method is always unfailingly carried out. The process of checking is a continuous one, but its aim is closer and closer approximation to a grasp of the total biblical data.

But could there be *timelessly eternal* affects in God? It is hard to see that there could be. For any change, from wrath to love, from self-sufficiency to self-giving, appears to pre-suppose or to imply a corresponding change in belief or knowledge. For it is the change in belief which gives to the emotional affect its distinctive character. Emotion is not just sensation; the fear of betrayal differs from the fear of war because of the different beliefs in each case.

If so, then a God who has (undergoes?) emotional changes (whether timelessly eternal or not) also has changes in belief or knowledge, and either was not or is not omniscient.

IV

Finally, some brief comments on the religious adequacy of the doctrine of divine impassibility. That doctrine is not a construct out of religious need, a postulate of the feeling

137

of absolute dependence, anymore than it is a derivation from the abstract idea of divine perfection.[11] Nor is religious adequacy a chief reason for accepting divine impassibility in the sense defined. But it is an *additional* reason; and certainly if divine impassibility were to turn out to be religiously deficient in some important way then that would be a good reason to re-consider the doctrine.

In Penelope Lively's novel *Moon Tiger* the main character, Claudia, has a daughter, Lisa. After an episode in which Claudia recalls incidents in Lisa's early life she has this to say:

> That Lisa – that Lisa unfettered by ignorance but also freed by it – is as dead now as ammonites and belemonites, as the figures in Victorian photographs, as the Plymouth settlers. Irretrievable also from the Lisa of today, who must grope with the rest of us for that distant self, that other self, that ephemeral teasing creature.

This passage brings out vividly the consequences of living in time and of changing; that there is a part of one's life which, at any given time, is irretrievably lost; that even while one lives, increasing parts of one's life are dead. That though one's knowledge may increase with time, more and more of one's life becomes inaccessible.

Part of what it means to say that God is immutable and therefore impassible is to deny such loss to God; there are not parts to God's life, parts which he has lived and which are accessible now only to memory; other parts which he has yet to live, accessible only in anticipation. That which is immutable and impassible is by nature complete. In

---

[11] For a defence of the importance of divine perfection in philosophical theology see 'Introduction' in *The Concept of God*, ed. T.V. Morris (Oxford, 1987).

Creel's words it 'must simply be, must be necessarily, completely and immediately possessed of the fullness of its being'.[12]

Given these consequences about divine immutability/impassibility, and other things about God – that he is supremely good and blessed, for example – it follows that God cannot change for the better or for the worse. He cannot change for the better, because he is already supremely good; he cannot change for the worse because he cannot be changed by anything.

It is difficult for us, for whom adaptability is in certain circumstances desirable, even a virtue, fully to comprehend that such changeableness would be a deficiency in the case of God. For such adaptability in God would betoken a prior need; the need to change in the light of new knowledge, or previous unpreparedness.

What are the religious or spiritual consequences of this? Briefly, I shall draw out two. The first is that such a God, and only such a God, can be known to be utterly reliable. This is something that the biblical writers focus upon. The writer of the Epistle to the Hebrews refers to the immutability of God's promises, and to the 'strong consolation' that reliance upon them can produce (6:18). A God who was subject to change from some external force or agency could not console his people in this unconditioned manner.

More generally, it is only to such a God that a person can offer that unreserved yielding of the self which is of the essence of religious devotion. If the life of the object of devotion were to be subject to change, then the character of the devotion would be – or ought to be – suitably conditioned or qualified. No doubt human devotion to God

---

12 Creel *op. cit.* p. 104.

139

is often conditioned or qualified, but the reason for this does not lie in a natural and proper prudence but in an inadequate grasp of God's immutability, or in a failure of nerve.

The second consequence has to do with praise. There are different concepts of praise; for example, praise for achievement, recognition of a goal that has been reached with difficulty, even against the odds. That is an element in Christian praise of Christ 'who has gotten for us the victory'. But praise can also be offered for what an individual is in himself, where questions of ease or difficulty in arriving at the state or nature do not arise. Such praise is central to Christian spirituality, the offering of praise to God for what he is in himself, for the sort of being that he is. Unlike any of his creatures God is not subject to change and is therefore the only appropriate recipient of the unreserved offering of such praise.

V

This paper may seem to be excessively negative, even grudging. In closing, it is possible to put the main thesis in a more positive form.

Necessarily, human beings experience emotions or passions as affects. (They are 'affections'). But it is conceivable that what are necessarily experienced by human beings as affects are, as a matter of logic, capable of being experienced, or possessed, in non-affective ways. A suggestion was made in the paper that this is true of states such as joy or delight. Suppose we call any such a state had by God a *themotion*. (A themotion X is as close as possible to the corresponding human emotion X except that it cannot be an affect). Nothing that has been said in this paper is a denial that God has all those themotions which are consistent with his moral character to an unsurpassed degree.